MENTAL PATIENTS
AND SOCIAL NETWORKS

MENTAL PATIENTS
AND
SOCIAL NETWORKS

ROBERT PERRUCCI
DENA B. TARG
Purdue University

AH *Auburn House Publishing Company*
Boston, Massachusetts

Library of Congress Cataloging in Publication Data

Perrucci, Robert
 Mental patients and social networks.

 Includes index.
  1. Psychology, Pathological—Social aspects.
 2. Social psychiatry. I. Targ, Dena B. II. Title.
 [DNLM: 1. Mental disorders. 2. Social environment.
 3. Hospitals, Psychiatric. WM 31 P461m]
 RC455.P437   362.2′042   81-20630
 ISBN 0-86569-095-2   AACR2

Printed in the United States of America

PREFACE

This book has its intellectual roots in three distinct literatures. The first was initiated by the early writings of John Clausen and Marian Yarrow, who sought to understand the career of the mental patient as it was shaped within the social structure of the family. The second can be traced to the bold formulations of Thomas Scheff, who challenged the medical model of mental illness by emphasizing the social construction of mental illness. The third literature deals with the nature, properties, and significance of social networks and was introduced by Elizabeth Bott, J.A. Barnes, and J. Clyde Mitchell. Since these early writings, all three of these literatures have had considerable theoretical and empirical development upon which we have also tried to draw.

Our primary theoretical concern is to apply structural analysis consistently, as expressed in social network theory, to a problem that has ordinarily been pursued by studying the psychological or social characteristics of individuals. Our guiding theoretical assumption is that by studying the social networks in which patients are involved, much can be learned about how people become mental patients and what happens to them once they are patients. Thus, we study social networks in order to understand what happens to mental patients.

In carrying out this research we decided on intensive analysis of a small number of patients and their social networks in order to discover the social processes at work in defining people as mentally ill and to understand how these processes are viewed by persons directly involved. Our intent was not to test but to offer hypotheses for consideration by other researchers and practitioners. We believe that the network perspective developed in this book, and some of the substantive hypotheses offered for understanding the career of the mental patient, can be extended to other questions of theoretical and social significance, as, for example, the treatment of the aged in

American society. In addition, conceptualizing society as a web of interconnected social and organizational networks would do much to counter the individualism that dominates the theory and method of contemporary social science.

In this book we explore the process of becoming and being a mental patient from information obtained from hospital records of forty-seven patients committed to two large state mental hospitals and from approximately two hundred members of the social networks from which these patients came. Chapter 1 begins with an exposition and criticism of dominant approaches to the study of mental illness—the psychiatric model and the societal reaction model. The social network approach followed in this book is then presented as an alternative, with the focus on two central ideas. The first is an emphasis on the *process*—being defined as mentally ill, being hospitalized for that illness, and being declared as mentally restored and released from hospitalization. The second is the view that *social networks* are an important element in shaping the careers of mental patients. Our central theoretical argument is that much more can be learned about the process of becoming defined and treated as mentally ill by studying patients' social networks than by studying patients' psychological or social characteristics.

Chapter 2 discusses the procedures used to develop the typology of patients, which serves as the basis for analysis throughout the book. The forty-seven hospitalized persons are classified according to their committing symptoms and their status resources. Those committed for medical-psychiatric symptoms are classified as "patients," while those who violated social standards are called "deviants." Those who are married, employed, and better educated are viewed as having resources and are classified as "protected"; those with fewer resources are considered to be "vulnerable." Cross-classifying these characteristics produces our four patient types: Vulnerable Patients, Vulnerable Deviants, Protected Patients, and Protected Deviants.

Chapter 3 addresses patients' social networks and the way in which these networks react to the initial unusual behaviors exhibited by pre-patients. This material, which constitutes the first stage in the career of the mental patient, permits examination of the question of how different kinds of social networks attribute different meanings to early signs of unusual behavior and undertake different actions in response to them. Of particular interest are the size and composition of social networks, the density of ties among members, the closeness of ties to the patient and among network members, the extent to which networks are open to nonfamily members, and the structure of leadership within a network. Chapter 3 also examines the tendency of social networks to "medicalize" or "normalize" patients in response to initial unusual behaviors, revealed in the way in which initial unusual behaviors are described and explained. In addition, the chapter also explores whether or not a network seeks professional assistance for its troubled member.

Chapter 4 focuses on the network's decision to hospitalize one of its members. It is expected that before hospitalization occurs there will be some tendency to stabilize the deviant role of the pre-patient. Deviants will come to accept the definition of their unusual behaviors as an "illness" that requires the care or treatment of psychiatric personnel and facilities. In addition to the patient's role in the commitment decision, Chapter 4 examines the way that critical incidents or events (e.g., death of family member, divorce) that affect the social network can initiate consideration of commitment. This line of analysis seems most appropriate to understanding the situation of pre-patients whose problems have persisted for many years and to which their social networks have apparently adapted.

With hospitalization comes the direct, full-time involvement of psychiatric professionals in the patient's life. An official record, which is intended to document the onset, course, and treatment of the patient's illness, is established and maintained. The unofficial function of the hospital record is to legitimate the commitment decision made by the social network. However, the hospital also has the power, through its own definitions of the patient's illness, to determine the patient's future. Chapter 5 looks at the hospital phase in the career of the mental patient. Patients' hospital records are examined in an effort to disclose what is selected from a patient's past problems or family history for inclusion in the official record. The material selected by hospital representatives can lead to a very favorable or unfavorable prognosis for recovery or release. Special attention is directed to differences in records for different types of patients and to a comparison of the social network's view of a patient's illness with the view contained in the hospital record.

Chapter 6 compares the hospital experience of different types of patients and explores the relationship between patient types and their basic treatment program, either medical-psychiatric therapy or social control. The network's response to hospitalization in terms of "second thoughts" about the commitment and their potential for abandoning the patient is also examined. In addition, the relationship between patient types, social network characteristics, and continued contact with the patient (e.g., hospital visits, patient leaves, and home visits) is analyzed. Also considered in this chapter is the final stage in the patient's career: release or continued hospitalization. A comparison of patients who are released with those still hospitalized is carried out with respect to the four patient types and the characteristics of social networks. We show how network differences in the commitment process are related to a network's receptivity to have the patient back from the hospital. The final chapter summarizes the main findings of the book and discusses their theoretical and practical implications.

Our overriding purpose in writing this book is to illustrate the significance of social networks as the appropriate unit of analysis for understanding certain social phenomena. This purpose coincides with a growing theoretical and practical interest in the role of social support groups and networks as they affect individual and family functioning in dealing with the psychosocial stress of everyday life. While we applaud the greater attention being given to social networks and social support groups in academic and policy circles, we wish to offer a word of concern about the basis for this interest and a recommendation to others concerning future work in this area.

Interest in the role of social support groups and "natural" helping networks, especially in connection with the aged and mental health, occurs at a time when political decisionmakers are sharply reducing funds for human services. While agencies that assist more vulnerable segments of our society are being dismantled, interest in identifying social support groups and learning about how they assist their members *without* the aid of community professionals and federal dollars is increasing. One gets the impression that social support groups and "natural" helping networks that increase people's ability to "cope" with their situation are seen as effective alternatives to aid programs supported with public funds.

It would be unfortunate, indeed, if there were to develop some romantic notion about the unique capacity of "natural" helping groups to provide what people in trouble really need to get by. Helping groups *are* important, but their capacity to assist troubled members is also dependent on their own economic and social well-being. Social networks composed of persons with low-paying, insecure jobs, facing increasing inflation and an uncertain economy, will be no more able to assist troubled members than they are able to assist themselves. Moreover, most people—individuals or social networks—who turn to social service agencies probably do so because of the absence of a social network or because of the inadequacy of the social network to solve a problem.

Undoubtedly the size, cost, and consequences of the social service bureaucracy in the United States need to be reassessed. But to withdraw this source of support for individuals and for networks without a thoroughgoing analysis of how it is to be replaced would be, at the very least, irresponsible and, at the most, devastating to the people it is supposed to help. It is clearly akin to an analysis of the cost and consequences of institutionalization of the mentally ill, which concludes that because of the cost and negative consequences of hospitalization patients should be turned out to the street to fend for themselves.

The political decisions made at federal, state, and local levels to dismantle the infrastructure of economic and social services to low-income citizens will simultaneously increase the vulnerability of troubled citizens and reduce the capacity of support groups to assist them. Helping networks and support groups are not alternatives to publicly funded help programs, but are themselves in need of assistance in order that they may aid their more troubled members. The effectiveness of helping networks and support groups is often contingent on access to more advantaged individuals, professionals, and organizations with specialized resources and/or funds. At a time of shrinking services, informal helping networks will have fewer such individuals on whom to draw.

Genuine strengths have always existed among economically disadvantaged working-class men, women, and children in this society. However, we should avoid turning those strengths into caricatures of self-sufficient "natural" people who are spared the intrusions of government in their lives. The gap between encouraging strong social networks and withdrawing the services on which individuals and families have come to depend continues to widen. After all, there can be few viable "natural" helping groups in communities where one fourth of the adult males and females and one half of the teenagers are unemployed.

Finally, the theoretical importance of the study of social networks should be placed in proper perspective. A focus on social networks as the unit of analysis has major advantages over frameworks that concentrate on individual attributes. However, such a focus can also inhibit a consideration of larger political and economic structures. A focus on social networks often influences researchers to pay attention to which types of social networks are more or less able to help a troubled individual cope with such problems as unemployment or mental illness. Attention to coping behavior may discourage examination of the conditions that cause these problems in the first place.

It should hardly bear restatement that many of the social problems with which individuals and networks struggle to cope will only be completely solved through large-scale social change. We share with many others the constant tension between believing that major social change is necessary to solve many social problems and trying to assist those experiencing the individual effects of social problems. This dilemma is very real for many academics and human service professionals. As activist scholars our resolution is to simultaneously work to further social change whenever we can and to assist those who suffer under present social conditions.

ROBERT PERRUCCI

DENA B. TARG

ACKNOWLEDGMENTS

We would first like to thank the National Institute of Mental Health for a grant (USPHS-MH15790) in support of this research. Dena Targ also acknowledges the support of the Agricultural Experiment Station, Purdue University.

This project required the assistance of many people for its successful completion. During the first year our colleague Carolyn Cummings Perrucci played an important role in the construction of the final research design and in the development of data-collection instruments.

Once the design was established, the project benefited from dedicated and skillful interviewers. Special thanks is extended to John Meluch, whose perseverance in tracking down network members and sensitivity in interviewing them provided stability to data-collection activities. He was ably assisted by Leanor Johnson, Homer LaRue, Michael Ledvina, Enid Reichard, and Steven Wallach. Preparation of the data through cleaning, coding, and storage activities was the responsibility of Rose Haberer, Lorna Myers, and Vathsala Venugopolan. Bill Whitson developed special computer programs to handle some of the unique problems of network analysis we encountered.

The dedication of Cathy Alexander to this project was expressed in the hundreds of hours she devoted to reading and recording hospital records and to transcribing tapes of interviews with network members. Mary Perigo and Jean Greives ably transformed numerous working drafts into final manuscript form.

Finally, we would like to thank Carolyn C. Perrucci and Harry R. Targ who, although busy with their own work, always had the time to be supportive of ours.

R.P.
D.B.T.

CONTENTS

Chapter 1

PERSPECTIVES ON MADNESS: DISEASE, DEVIANCE, AND SOCIAL NETWORKS

"Lunacy." "Madness." "Mental illness." "Problems with living." Each of these terms has at one time or another been used to describe persons whose pattern of thought and behavior has been viewed by society as different, problematic, or requiring some special attention. Each term also represents a different point of view on the nature of the condition described and on the moral status of the afflicted person. In different times and places prevailing beliefs have viewed the disordered mind as something inflicted upon "sinners" who had transgressed moral codes, "casualties" of a changing social order, "patients" who had contracted a disease, or "victims" who had suffered from economic deprivation.

During the past twenty years there has been a vigorous effort in medical and social science circles to increase understanding of mental illness and to clarify the reasons for psychiatric hospitalization. Most writing on the subject, including research and theoretical work, has been based in two opposing perspectives. The first is generally referred to as a *medical* or *psychiatric* perspective because of its emphasis on mental illness as a "disease." Persons afflicted with the "disease" are viewed as incapacitated or as experiencing restricted performance. If their illness comes to the attention of medical-psychiatric professionals and they are hospitalized for treatment, they become *patients*.

Advocates of the second perspective emphasize the way in which persons and groups react to deviant behavior that results in someone

1

being defined as mentally ill and being hospitalized. Because of the emphasis on how people react to and define the behavior of others, this view has been referred to as the *societal reaction* perspective. Persons who become mental patients start out as *deviants,* who may be no more incapacitated than other persons who do not become patients. What sets deviants apart is a set of social characteristics and circumstances that increase the likelihood of their behavior being viewed as mental illness and of their being hospitalized. These social characteristics, including, for example, a person's marital status, employment status, and education, have positive and negative social connotations. Social characteristics, with positive connotations, serve as resources that people can use to their advantage. For example, a married person may have social and emotional resources to call upon, and employment may provide a person with economic resources as well as with evidence of being able to meet responsibilities. Social circumstances also include such factors as whether a person's deviance is exhibited in public and whether it comes to the attention of officials such as police, social workers, or medical personnel.

This chapter examines the main features of the two perspectives on the nature of mental illness and provides some detailed comparisons between them. The chapter also contains a general critique of the medical and societal reaction perspectives as a basis for introducing an alternative—namely, a *social network* perspective on the process of being defined as mentally ill and being hospitalized for that illness.

Medical-Psychiatric Perspective

The medical-psychiatric perspective starts with the view that mental illness exists as a dysfunction of the mind and manifests itself in clearly discernible symptoms: unusual, bizarre, disoriented, or peculiar behavior that can be diagnosed and has a typical onset, course, and outcome. In theory the symptoms of mental disorder are culture-free, in much the same way that pneumonia has a universal symptomatology.

Within the medical-psychiatric perspective there are different conceptualizations of mental illness and how it is manifested. Consider, for example, the following summary of conditions felt to be indicative of mental illness:

It is becoming increasingly apparent that modes of conceptualizing mental illness refer to any of four conditions: (1) the experience of severe and prolonged subjective distress; (2) necessary undesirable concomitants or sequelae of such severe and prolonged subjective distress (e.g., tissue damage or cognitive disorientation); (3) the inability to adapt to, cope with, or defend against potentially stress-inducing circumstances; and (4) the adoption of patterns of response to severe and prolonged distress regarded as intrinsically undesirable and/or viewed as having the undesirable consequences of impeding normal role performance or as being otherwise disruptive of group functioning (e.g., autistic withdrawal, paranoid ideation, hallucinatory behavior, alcohol abuse, and anti-social behavior).[1]

One version of the medical-psychiatric model (the medical emphasis) deals with disturbances that can be traced to genetic, biological, or toxic origins. It is generally conceded in such cases that the disease does indeed reside in the body in much the same fashion as pneumonia. However, a second version of the model (the psychiatric emphasis) deals with functional disorders for which there is no known organic cause. According to this version, psychiatric symptoms reflecting a functional disorder are revealed by the behavior, thought patterns, and emotional state of an individual. Such symptoms can be elicited in extensive clinical examination or through use of short screening devices in household interviews.[2] Functional disorders, reflected in behavioral and ideational symptoms, affect the largest proportion of persons identified as mentally ill and are the major concern of this book.[3]

In trying to understand the etiology of mental illness, proponents of the psychiatric version of the medical-psychiatric model give special attention to social factors. Early ecological studies of the spatial distribution of schizophrenia found that the highest rates of admissions for mental illness were concentrated in the slum areas of cities.[4] Such studies led to the conclusion that the social disorganization in deteriorating areas helped to produce a disordered personality. More recent research has continued to develop theoretical explanations for the cause of psychopathology that emphasize social and cultural factors. Mental illness has been viewed as causally linked to social isolation, to the stresses produced by economic deprivation, to the inability of persons in lower social classes to deal with stress, and to the tensions and frustrations of the female role.[5] The core theoretical argument in all of this research is that psychological stress is socially induced by socioeconomic deprivations and by social roles that block or frustrate aspirations.

Attempts have been made to combine the medical and psychiatric views of mental illness into a single theory that would help to explain the recurrent finding that rates of schizophrenia are highest in the lowest socioeconomic strata. One hypothesis is that the interaction of genetic vulnerability (medical perspective) and impaired ability to deal with stress (psychiatric perspective) results in higher rates of schizophrenia in the lower class.[6] Briefly put, the argument is that persons in the lower classes (1) have a greater genetic susceptibility to schizophrenia, (2) experience a greater number of stress-producing circumstances (ill health, economic insecurity, over-crowding, degradation), and (3) are poorly equipped by family socialization to deal with social stress.

Other attempts to explain the relationship between socio-economic status and mental illness have suggested a broad "sociomedical formulation" that links medical and social influences.[7] Socioeconomic factors can affect mental illness through direct influence on physiological symptoms. For example, persons from lower-status backgrounds may have greater exposure to infectious diseases that are responsible for schizophrenia and brain disorders. Socioeconomic factors may also mediate the effect of infectious diseases (and other biological factors) by their effect on preventive care. Lower-status persons may hold attitudes toward health care that inhibit them from seeking medical attention that would minimize the negative effects of infectious diseases. Thus, Rushing and Ortega call for "the integration of medical and sociological factors in a common (sociomedical) interpretation [of mental illness]."[8]

Whatever the differences between the medical and psychiatric models, the medical-psychiatric perspective is unified by the view that the behaviors exhibited by persons hospitalized for mental illness represent serious pathology. For example, in reviewing evidence from studies of how the mentally ill are identified, Walter Gove states: "In sum, the evidence strongly suggests that persons, typically, are hospitalized because they have an active psychiatric disorder which is extremely difficult for themselves and/or others to handle."[9] Gove also assumes the existence of a careful and rigorous review process for potential patients so that persons eventually hospitalized exhibit problems sharply differentiated from both the "normal" population and persons with only "moderate" psychiatric symptoms. Gove continues:

> *The vast majority of persons who become patients have a serious disturbance, and it is only when the situation becomes untenable that*

action is taken. The public officials who perform the major screening role do not simply process all of the persons who come before them as mentally ill but instead screen out a large portion. If the person passes this initial screening, he will probably be committed, and there is reason to assume the process at this point frequently becomes somewhat ritualized. But even here a number of persons are released either through the psychiatric examination or the court hearing.[10]

Critics of the medical-psychiatric model have raised questions about the assumption that the behavior of mentally ill persons represents serious psychiatric symptoms. It has been suggested that hospital psychiatrists' diagnoses of acts of deviance invariably exaggerate the degree of severity and the seriousness of the behavior in question. A prevailing "medical ideology," with its concept of illness, tends to legitimatize a particular view of disease that is "embedded in the historical and cultural present of the white middle class of Western societies."[11]

An added difficulty with the medical-psychiatric view of mental illness is that it draws heavily for evidence of the concept of "disorder" or "illness" from persons admitted into psychiatric treatment. Dependence upon evidence drawn from treated cases of illness may present a very distorted picture of psychiatric symptoms that exaggerates differences between persons being treated and the general population.

Attempts to measure both treated and untreated cases of mental illness, and thereby to obtain a measure of true prevalence, have not really improved our knowledge of the types of behavior that should be included under the term "mental illness." This lack of knowledge is primarily due to the procedures used to collect symptom information as well as the procedures used to make diagnostic judgements of that information.[12]

Thus, three questions central to the medical-psychiatric perspective remain open: (1) What behavior should be viewed as indicative of "mental illness" or "psychopathology"? (2) Are the behaviors exhibited by patients substantially different from those exhibited by "normals"? (3) Are the behaviors exhibited by patients so severe as to require hospitalization?

Societal Reaction Perspective

The societal reaction approach to understanding mental illness shifts attention away from the psychiatric symptoms that are held to be indicative of mental disorder, and the physical and social causes of those symptoms, to the rule-making and deviance-defining actions of social groups. Persons are classified as mentally ill because their conduct has been defined as having violated certain rules of appropriate behavior.

Some of the central features of the societal reaction perspective are found in the work of Edwin Lemert and Howard Becker, who were concerned with the nature of deviance.[13] Lemert, for example, drew the very important distinction between primary and secondary deviation. *Primary deviation* includes a wide variety of deviant acts having only marginal implication for the psychological structure of individuals; *secondary deviation* is behavior that constitutes the adaptation an individual makes to deal with the problems resulting from reactions to the primary deviation. Secondary deviation, which is socially created, probably constitutes the bulk of the behavior for which persons come into conflict with social control agencies.

When applied to mental illness, the societal reaction perspective challenges the view that most cases of mental illness are the result of an underlying disease that sharply differentiates persons with and without a mental illness. In particular, advocates of the societal reaction perspective are skeptical about whether the behaviors exhibited by most hospitalized persons reflect a serious disturbance that can be traced to underlying psychological causes. Instead, the perspective is based on the view that large segments of a population, at one time or another, engage in acts of primary deviation (i.e., rule breaking). Some acts of primary deviation have well-established labels for the violations and are therefore understood—for example, a "drinking problem." However, society has no agreed-upon labels for many violations of social codes, which are therefore not understood. Mental illness, according to Thomas Scheff, is a catch-all category of residual rule violations for which there are no conventional terms of explanation: "If people reacting to an offense exhaust the conventional categories that might define it (e.g., theft, prostitution, drunkenness), yet are certain that an offense has been committed, they may resort to this residual category. In earlier societies, the residual category was witchcraft, spirit possession, or possession by the devil; today it is mental illness. The symptoms of mental illness are, therefore, violations of residual rules."[14]

Since a substantial proportion of rulebreakers are in the nonhospitalized population, the central question posed by the societal reaction perspective is: What differentiates rulebreakers who become classified as mentally ill and hospitalized from rulebreakers who do not? Attempts to answer this question have focused upon a number of circumstances that can influence societal reactions to rulebreakers—namely, the characteristics (e.g., level of education) of the social groups in which the rulebreakers are located, the education, occupation, or income of the rulebreakers, and the social setting in which the rule breaking takes place.[15]

The process of becoming defined as mentally ill covers a wide range of events that begin with rule breaking and end with hospitalization. Each stage in the process, as well as the experience of persons moving through the process, has been examined by a number of researchers, who have attempted to identify the effect that different circumstances and social conditions have on the likelihood of one's being defined as mentally ill, being hospitalized, or being released from a hospital. For example, research evidence indicates that (1) the presence of legal counsel at admission hearings sharply reduces the probability of commitment; (2) there is a conservative bias in psychiatric decision making that presumes illness even when considerable uncertainty exists about how dangerous or impaired a patient may be; (3) persons with limited education and income have higher rates of involuntary commitment; and (4) the likelihood of being released from a mental hospital is influenced by social factors that have little to do with judgements about the psychopathology of patients.[16]

Although the existence of evidence about the effect of social factors on hospitalization increases the plausibility of the societal reaction perspective, serious questions remain concerning the validity of the perspective in comparison to a medical-psychiatric view of mental illness. For example, Rushing, who uses a societal reaction perspective in much of his research on mental illness, cautions against overemphasizing the importance of social factors in the hospitalization decision. His caution is based on the fact that many studies based on the societal reaction perspective make no attempt to determine whether there is evidence of behavior pathology among persons who have been committed. Thus, we do not know whether persons of low socioeconomic status are more often committed because of societal reaction to their low status or because low status is correlated with severe behavior pathology.

There have been a number of important critiques of the societal reaction perspective.[17] Contrary to the hypotheses and evidence put forward by proponents of the perspective, Gove argues that (1) persons hospitalized for mental illness exhibit serious behavior pathology; (2) the process associated with hospitalization for mental illness is one of persistent denial of the illness and avoidance of affixing the label "mentally ill" rather than a quick and easy commitment; and (3) persons with greater social and economic resources are more likely (not less likely, as predicted by the societal reaction perspective) to seek out psychiatric treatment, including hospitalization.

Efforts to assess the weight of existing evidence or to provide new evidence bearing on the relative validity of the medical-psychiatric and societal reaction perspectives provide inconclusive results. A review of the evidence from eighteen studies specifically concerned with hypotheses derived from a societal reaction perspective shows that thirteen provide support for the perspective while five do not.[18] However, firm conclusions would require a closer examination of the methodology and samples of the studies being compared. Rushing has provided the best assessment of the importance, in the hospitalization process, of an individual's resources as measured by educational and marital status in comparison to the assessed level of impairment on admission.[19] Rushing's studies conclude that a patient's resources have a clear effect upon the hospitalization process; patients with fewer resources are more likely to undergo court commitment than voluntary commitment. More importantly, Rushing finds considerable interaction between a patient's resources and the degree of psychiatric impairment, in that the effect of a patient's resources upon the type of commitment is modified when the judged level of impairment involves extremely disruptive and bizarre symptoms. Thus, Rushing concludes that people are hospitalized both because they are severely ill *and* because they have limited resources.

One should approach Rushing's conclusions with caution when trying to assess the importance of his research in resolving the competing views of the medical-psychiatric and the societal reaction perspectives. Most questionable, perhaps, is his use of official hospital records to estimate the severity or seriousness of the patient's symptoms on admission. Whether official diagnoses are accurate reflections of events in a pre-patient's life or simply after-the-fact justifications of a decision made on other grounds is an empirical question of considerable importance. An added problem, which Rushing acknowledges, is the examination of only the influence of a patient's educational and marital resources on the hospitalization process. Other resources may be of greater importance in keeping people with problems out of the hospital.

Limitations of the Medical-Psychiatric and Societal Reaction Perspectives

It is apparent from the preceding sections that neither the medical-psychiatric nor the societal reaction perspective provides unambiguous findings with respect to key hypotheses about why people are hospitalized for mental illness. Unresolved questions remain concerning the behavior of persons who are defined as mentally ill and are hospitalized. Questions also remain concerning particular social factors, apart from any unusual, serious, or problematic behaviors, that are expected to influence the hospitalization process.

The questions dividing the two perspectives, which have dominated theory and research for almost two decades, may never be resolved with the research strategies and data sources in current use. Following are four overriding problems with the theoretical and methodological approaches of the two perspectives.

Lack of Emphasis on Illness as a Sequence of Stages

With a few notable exceptions, most of the theoretical and empirical work dealing with mental illness has either neglected to consider more than one stage in the "career" of the mental patient or has focused primarily on the decision to hospitalize.[20] The career of the mental patient should be viewed as including a sequence of interrelated stages and processes that begins with the recognition of unusual and problematic behaviors and continues through the individual's becoming a patient and then a non-patient again.

The special attention given to the hospitalization decision (e.g., type of commitment, severity of committing symptoms, court proceedings) is understandable because of the easy availability of data on these events. However, before we can view either the medical-psychiatric or the societal reaction perspective as the better theory, we must demonstrate that the perspective in question improves our understanding of what happens to people once they are hospitalized, whether and under what conditions they are released, and what factors affect posthospital adjustment.

Use of a career approach to mental illness will require research that follows patients over time as they proceed through different stages, as well as research that follows up on former patients.[21]

Overemphasis on Hospital Records as a Source of Data

A large body of existing research on hospitalization for mental illness has relied upon official hospital records as a main source of data. Intake interviews by hospital staff or statements by attending physicians in court commitments have been used to determine the severity of symptoms, the onset of illness, the time when symptoms were first noticed, and the patient's relationships with family members. Existing research has also largely accepted as a valid indicator of very different admission patterns the hospital classification of patients as voluntary or involuntary admissions. Researchers have viewed persons admitted to hospitals on a voluntary commitment as having been spared the public pressure and the stigma associated with involuntary commitment.[22] Voluntary admissions have also been viewed as better risks for therapy and release.[23] In short, researchers have commonly accepted voluntary hospitalization as self-recognition of incapacitating or problematic symptoms and have not attributed these admissions to a negative reaction on the part of society to people with limited resources.

Given that mental hospitals are formal organizations, it is plausible that an organization's official description of events experienced by clients would not necessarily correspond to the descriptions offered by the clients themselves. Moreover, the extent of correspondence between what family, friends, and acquaintances say about a patient's behavior and what eventually appears in hospital records remains a question to be answered by research. For some types of symptoms or diagnosis, there may be a close correspondence between what people close to a patient say and what hospital records contain about his or her life history or events. In other cases, there may be little correspondence. Thus, one should be skeptical about accepting without evidence the validity of official hospital data on admitting symptoms or type of admission. Discrepancies may be expected because of a hospital's tendency to select information that corresponds to its own working conceptions of health and illness and because of the tendency of psychiatric professionals to make judgements about illness that are influenced by extraneous factors.[24]

It is also possible that patients officially classified as voluntary admissions may have experienced the same degree of coercion and public labeling as have involuntary admissions.[25] Some patients may, in effect, have been given a choice by their family that they either commit themselves (for convenience) or the family will seek a court commitment. In such a circumstance the important theoretical distinction between a voluntary and an involuntary admission is diminished.[26]

Reliance upon a Single Informant

Some researchers have chosen not to use official hospital data when studying the commitment process and have instead relied upon information provided by a member of the patient's social network.[27] Generally, the patient's spouse, closest relative, or other committing party has served as the researcher's informant concerning the patient's unusual or bizarre behavior or the decision to hospitalize.

Data obtained in this fashion avoid some of the problems associated with overemphasis on the hospital record, but it is not an entirely satisfactory alternative. Prior to hospitalization, a pre-patient may be involved in frequent relationships with family members, co-workers, or neighbors. Rather than rely on the recollections of only one of these persons, researchers would obtain more valid information if all members of a patient's social network are asked about initial symptoms, perceived seriousness of the symptoms, degree of family disruption caused by the pre-patient, or perceived need for hospitalization.

There may be much or little correspondence among the views of persons involved with the patient. The degree of consensus or dissent in a patient's social network is not simply a measure of the reliability or validity of the information obtained from respondents. The degree of agreement among network members on certain matters may be an important influence on the commitment process. The degree of agreement may also influence the extent to which the network remains accessible to a hospitalized person, as well as the network's receptivity to accepting the patient after release.

Distortion of the Significance of Patient Symptoms and Resources

The key factors in both the medical-psychiatric perspective (the seriousness of psychiatric symptoms) and the societal reaction perspective (the patient's social and economic resources) have been treated in a fashion that may distort their significance in the everyday lives of the pre-patient and his or her social network. For example, studies that use psychiatric symptoms as part of their explanatory framework invariably use either the official diagnosis (schizophrenia, neurosis, personality disorder) or the degree of psychological impairment (severe, moderate, mild) as the measure of symptom severity. The problem with this procedure is that if one develops a list of symptoms exhibited by pre-patients before hospitalization, the list will cover dozens of behaviors that could easily be classified in several diagnostic and symptom-severity categories. In effect, one has made a selection, from a long list of possible symptoms, that will serve as the dominant characterization of a patient's psychopathology. Why one particular type of symptom is selected for official diagnosis is not clear. Is it the most serious symptom? Is it the most frequently repeated symptom? Is it an overriding symptom from which others are derived? Until there is some answer to such questions, the use of official data on symptoms and diagnosis will be suspect.

In the same way, research that explains hospital commitment on the basis of an abundance or deficiency of social resources has generally focused upon amount of education, type of occupation, employment, income, and marital status as measures of resources. Particular resources are often selected for consideration without a clear rationale. Different researchers may use different resources, and at times the same researcher will use one resource in one study and a different one in a later study. The different social and economic resources are obviously treated as equivalent in terms of their expected effect on hospitalization. But it would seem that if a social or economic resource is supposed to influence one's family, friends, or the community at large to produce a positive or negative societal reaction, then the significance of that resource must be understood within the social network that is presumably responding to the resource. For example, having a high school diploma may be a positive resource if all other members of the social network never went beyond sixth grade. However, the same diploma might not be viewed as a positive resource if all other network members were college graduates. In sum, if social and economic resources are to be considered as a theoretically important factor in the hospitalization process, then the resources should be linked to the social context in which the pre-patient lives and works.

Paths to and from the Mental Hospital: A Social Network Approach

To avoid many of the problems of the competing perspectives we have discussed, we follow an approach to understanding mental illness that focuses on several central ideas. First is a focus on the *process* of becoming defined as mentally ill, hospitalized for that illness, and redefined as no longer mentally ill and released from hospitalization. Focusing on mental illness as a process requires the identification of the stages in the career of the mental patient and on the particular social mechanisms that facilitate movement from one stage to another. The stages in the process of becoming "mentally ill" and becoming "normal" again are interrelated. Each stage in the patient's career results in changes in the attitude, expectations, and behavior of all persons in the social network (including the patient). People do not become identified as mentally ill overnight. Often a sequence of events covering a long period of time is involved in redefining a "mean" or "ill-tempered" person as someone who is "dangerous," "sick," or "mentally ill." Still other sequences of events must enter into the decision to hospitalize a person for the newly recognized illness. Such decisions may not occur as an immediate response to some unusual, bizarre, or dangerous behavior but may be shaped by forces and circumstances about which very little is known.

Conceptualizing the process of becoming mentally ill as a career may lead to the uncovering of similarities with life cycle changes. The life cycle has clearly marked events and rituals (e.g., graduation, marriage) that serve as transition points to a new stage, "announcements" that individuals must now be treated differently—that is, in accordance with the expectations reserved for married persons or high school graduates.

The second idea on which we focus is the *social network*, a set of direct and indirect ties among a defined group of persons. The configuration of linkages, as well as their content, has consequences for members of the network. Thus, the social network out of which a patient comes may be composed of immediate family, relatives, co-workers, neighbors, and acquaintances. Not all of these persons may have direct links with all the others, but the sum total of direct and indirect ties constitutes the social network.

Network analysis is concerned with examining how specific properties of social networks can affect the behavior of persons embedded in them. In the present study we attempt to identify properties of social networks and explain how they influence the movement of patients from one stage to another. Each stage represents a critical point in the experiences of the deviant/patient and of his or her social network. The actions of the deviant/patient, and the response to those actions by the network, influence movement from one stage to another and may increase the likelihood of hospitalization. Similarly, the hospital's response to the patient and his or her social network results in an official description of the patient's problem, a prognosis for improvement, and a plan of therapy/custody. The hospital's construction of reality will influence the network's view of the patient's problem and shape its collective judgement about the patient's future.

Social networks have for some time been recognized as important factors in influencing psychological problems and hospitalization. Some researchers have considered social networks a "cause" of mental disorder and have suggested that persons who are alienated from their social networks are more likely to exhibit psychosocial impairment.[28] However, it is much more useful to look at social networks as factors that mediate between initial unusual behaviors (or symptoms) and the ways in which they are defined, explained, and acted upon. Over twenty-five years ago attention was given to this aspect of social networks by John Clausen, Marian Yarrow, and their associates.[29] Since that time other researchers have also noted how selected aspects of the social networks in which pre-patients are found can influence the likelihood that pre-patients will be hospitalized for mental illness or will find their way to psychiatric treatment or health professionals.[30]

Having hypothesized that the properties of a social network will influence the behavior of its members, we must specify the particular properties that are of theoretical interest. Some guidance is provided by available conceptual and theoretical work on networks.[31] J. Clyde Mitchell, for example, identifies two characteristics of networks as *density* and *reachability*, which refer, respectively, to the number and pattern of links in the network and to the ease with which persons in the network can be contacted. In addition, Mitchell examines the nature of the links with reference to such concepts as the *content*, *directionality*, *intensity*, and *frequency* of their interactions.

The network properties in the present study are selected in terms of their relevance to events at different stages in the career of a mental patient. Different properties of social networks are related to the commitment process, to the maintenance of ties with patients, and to an early release. Allan Horwitz, for example, looks at the strength of ties in the kin network and involvement in an open friendship network as they influence referral to psychiatric agencies. He suggests that strong kin networks provide emotional support for members and create less reliance on professional helping agencies. On the other hand, he posits that open friendship networks provide more channels of information and more diverse information and thereby facilitate access to psychiatric agencies.[32]

One early study of the influence of network properties on hospitalization found that persons who are in a critical position in their network (i.e., their behavior is essential to network maintenance) are hospitalized more rapidly than those in noncritical positions. It was also found that patients with close, symmetrical ties are "more likely to receive personal care, help in the performance of tasks, attempts at non-hospital medical therapy and initiation of hospitalization by those close to them than were patients with less frequent contact and non-symmetrical ties."[33]

Figure 1.1 contains a summary of our general hypothesis concerning interrelated stages in the career of a mental patient and the role of social networks in facilitating or blocking movement from one stage to another. In the following sections we consider each of these stages and intervening processes in turn.

Stage One: Primary Deviation

From the point of view of the present research, the career of the mental patient begins with the first socially recognized unusual behaviors exhibited by the pre-patient. These behaviors, which ultimately become symptoms, may be extremely varied in content, timing, and location. The main concern with initial unusual behaviors is whether they can be "normalized" or explained with reference to nonmedical or nonpsychiatric knowledge, or whether they are so extreme or bizarre that only a medical-psychiatric explanation seems plausible. Implicit in this distinction is the belief that societal reaction to the initial unusual behaviors of the pre-patient will reflect varying degrees of certainty or ambiguity about how to account for what has happened.

A close examination of the initial unusual behaviors, and the certainty or ambiguity associated with a network's attempt to under-

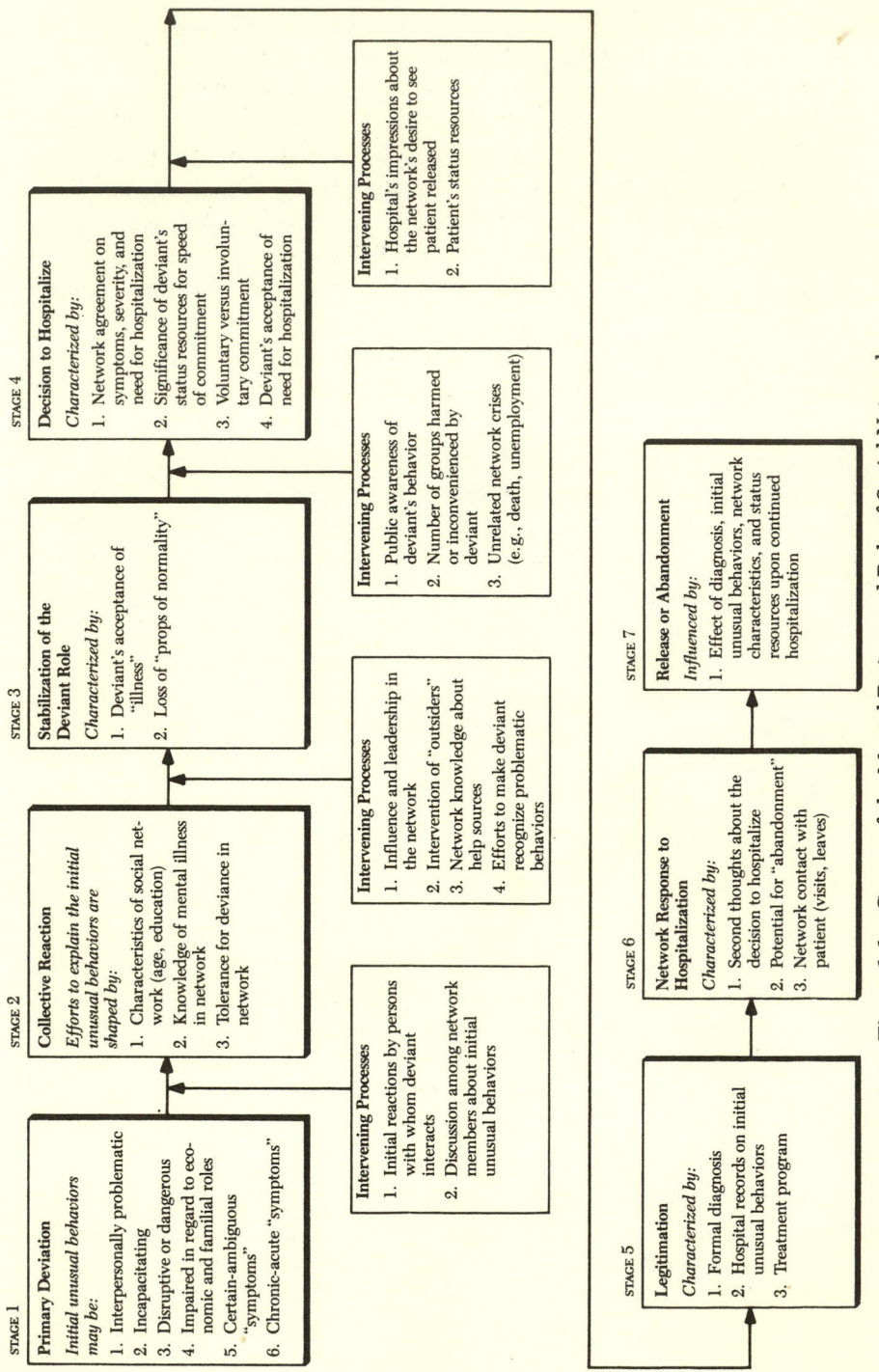

Figure 1.1 Career of the Mental Patient and Role of Social Networks.

STAGE 1

Primary Deviation

Initial unusual behaviors may be:

1. Interpersonally problematic
2. Incapacitating
3. Disruptive or dangerous
4. Impaired in regard to economic and familial roles
5. Certain-ambiguous "symptoms"
6. Chronic-acute "symptoms"

Intervening Processes

1. Initial reactions by persons with whom deviant interacts
2. Discussion among network members about initial unusual behaviors

STAGE 2

Collective Reaction

Efforts to explain the initial unusual behaviors are shaped by:

1. Characteristics of social network (age, education)
2. Knowledge of mental illness in network
3. Tolerance for deviance in network

Intervening Processes

1. Influence and leadership in the network
2. Intervention of "outsiders"
3. Network knowledge about help sources
4. Efforts to make deviant recognize problematic behaviors

STAGE 3

Stabilization of the Deviant Role

Characterized by:

1. Deviant's acceptance of "illness"
2. Loss of "props of normality"

Intervening Processes

1. Public awareness of deviant's behavior
2. Number of groups harmed or inconvenienced by deviant
3. Unrelated network crises (e.g., death, unemployment)

STAGE 4

Decision to Hospitalize

Characterized by:

1. Network agreement on symptoms, severity, and need for hospitalization
2. Significance of deviant's status resources for speed of commitment
3. Voluntary versus involuntary commitment
4. Deviant's acceptance of need for hospitalization

Intervening Processes

1. Hospital's impressions about the network's desire to see patient released
2. Patient's status resources

STAGE 5

Legitimation

Characterized by:

1. Formal diagnosis
2. Hospital records on initial unusual behaviors
3. Treatment program

STAGE 6

Network Response to Hospitalization

Characterized by:

1. Second thoughts about the decision to hospitalize
2. Potential for "abandonment"
3. Network contact with patient (visits, leaves)

STAGE 7

Release or Abandonment

Influenced by:

1. Effect of diagnosis, initial unusual behaviors, network characteristics, and status resources upon continued hospitalization

stand them, will help to answer a central question on which proponents of the medical-psychiatric and the societal reaction approaches disagree: Are the problematic behaviors of pre-patients indicative of severe mental disorders, or are they acts of deviance that can be subjected to interpretations other than medical-psychiatric?

Stage Two: Collective Reaction

After individually observing the initial unusual behaviors, members of a patient's social network will begin to share information about what they have observed and how they feel about it. In cases where the behaviors are quite varied, ranging from high to low degrees of perceived seriousness, the network has the option of choosing which initial unusual behaviors they will focus upon.

The choice of initial unusual behaviors of greater concern, and the explanation of those behaviors, will most likely be shaped by certain features of the social network. Networks with members who have more education and more knowledge of mental illness are more likely to select and explain symptoms in medical and psychiatric terms. Networks with greater tolerance for deviance are more likely to use nonmedical, nonpsychiatric explanations for the behavior. In networks where members frequently interact and where the network is perceived as emotionally "close," there should be more of an attempt to "normalize" the behavior or to handle it within the network.

During the collective reaction stage several processes may emerge that result in movement toward the next stage. The appearance of a key figure or leader in the social network can serve to crystallize reactions to the deviant very quickly. A strong opinion leader may be able to move the network to make a clear decision about the behavior network members have observed—that is, to view it as normal or as an example of mental illness. The intervention of an "outsider," especially a professional such as social worker or physician, will induce the network to "medicalize" rather than "normalize" the problematic behaviors. Professionals also are carriers of information about help sources in the community that may be drawn upon if needed.

Finally, it is expected that some networks, in the hope of finding a solution to the problem, will discuss matters with the deviant who exhibits problematic behaviors. In some cases discussion may simply be a call to "pull yourself together," while in others it may involve efforts to get the deviant "to see someone for help."

Stage Three: Stabilizing the Deviant Role

Before the career of the mental patient can continue to unfold, the position of the deviant in the network must be stabilized. That is, the deviant's behaviors must be repeated in regular fashion (or are at least so perceived), and associated role changes must reinforce the deviant role. For example, a pre-patient may stop working, stop normal household routines, or alter long-established social and interpersonal patterns. Such behavior has been referred to as a loss of the "props of normality," which increases movement toward the mental patient stage.

Several other processes may also intervene at this point. The unusual behaviors of the deviant may become more public, either because of actions by the deviant in public or because of network members who extend beyond the family or kin groups (e.g., co-workers). Additional problems may be created for the network because they must now try to explain to outsiders what has been going on with one of their members. Efforts to continue to "normalize" the unusual behaviors become more difficult as more persons or groups external to the network become involved.

There is also the possibility of unrelated and unanticipated events creating a new crisis for the network. For example, a death in the network, an economic setback like loss of a job (by the deviant or by some other member of the network), or a move to a new neighborhood may serve as a stimulant to the network to do something about its "old problem" (i.e., the long-standing problem of the deviant member).

Stage Four: Decision to Hospitalize

The first formal and public acknowledgment by the network that one of its members has a mental illness takes place with the decision to commit him or her to a mental hospital. The network's deviant is now a mental patient. Little is known about how, or how quickly, the decision to hospitalize is made (i.e., the time elapsed between Stage One and Stage Four). Networks will probably try to achieve some consensus on the need for hospitalization, especially if the initial unusual behaviors lacked certainty and clarity in medical or psychiatric terms. In cases of extremely bizarre or dangerous behavior, the decision to commit may proceed without any effort within the network to attain a consensus. It is also expected that networks will make some effort to get the deviant to accept the wisdom of the hospitalization decision and thereby not resist commitment.

Of special interest in the analysis of the decision to hospitalize is the relative importance of (1) the initial unusual behaviors, (2) the social and economic resources of the deviant, and (3) network consensus upon the speed with which hospitalization occurs and upon the type of commitment sought. It is expected that the manner in which these factors shape the decision to hospitalize also plays an important part in whether the patient ever leaves the hospital (Stage Seven).

Stage Five: Legitimation

Hospitalization brings with it the powers of the state and its agents of social control. If a patient enters the hospital via a court commitment, the hospital receives justification for the commitment in the form of official commitment proceedings and the statements of the committing party and attending physicians. In the case of a voluntary commitment, the hospital staff must justify the commitment on the basis of interviews with the patient and others, such as family members, physicians, or friends who may be involved.

In either case, the hospital obtains information on the initial unusual behaviors (and all other unusual behaviors) from several sources. The hospital also obtains a social history on the patient and his or her family from one or more sources. In this process the hospital staff forms its own impressions about the patient's illness (diagnosis and severity), the nature of its onset, and the type of treatment needed. In addition to impressions about the patient, the staff also forms impressions about the network, the patient's past role in the network, and what help the network could be to the patient in the future.

During this intake period the hospital is confronted with a great deal of information about the patient and the patient's social network. The staff makes choices about what should be included and what should be stressed as important. A patient's career in the hospital can be shaped in very different ways according to the kind of information that finds its way into a patient's formal record. If a patient's family is characterized by the intake interviewer as stable, supportive, and very interested in its member's welfare, that patient will have a very different hospital experience from the patient who is viewed as coming from a disturbed and fragmented family.

Thus, we are interested in the degree of agreement between what appears in a patient's hospital record and what network members say about the patient and about the strength of ties within the network. Agreement or disagreement may be related to network characteristics, patient symptoms, or patient status resources.

Stage Six: Network Response to Hospitalization

After hospitalization some networks will rethink the wisdom of the decision they have made. Doubts may develop about whether the hospitalized person really is mentally ill or really needs to be hospitalized. On the other hand, some networks may view the hospitalization as the best decision they have ever made. The absence of the disturbed and disturbing person may have brought more tranquility than the network has experienced for some time. Hospitalization may therefore be viewed as an opportunity for both the patient and the network to regain a level of stability.

The way in which a network assesses the decision they have recently made may influence whether they continue to maintain ties with the patient in terms of emotional bonds, visits to the hospital, and weekend leaves for the patient. Although many patients will be "defined away" as members of the network at the time of the decision to hospitalize, the actual abandonment process, if it does occur, will in most cases occur after hospitalization.

Stage Seven: Release or Abandonment

The final stage in the career of a mental patient is concerned with the patient's chances for an early release or for long-term institutionalization. The chances that a patient will be released are considerably better if people outside the hospital are actively seeking a release. The characteristics of a patient's social network may therefore be of considerable importance. It is also possible, however, that a patient's diagnosis and judged illness may be the overriding factors influencing release from the hospital.

Analysis of Data on Patients and Their Social Networks

The remainder of this book examines the process of becoming a mental patient. Data were obtained from official records concerning forty-seven patients committed to two large state mental hospitals and from interviews with approximately 200 members of the social networks from which the patients come (see Appendix C).

The first step was to develop a typology of patients that will serve as the basis for a comparative analysis of different types of patients. The basis for creating patient types was found in the key ideas of the two competing perspectives on mental illness discussed earlier. The medical-psychiatric approach emphasizes the severity of debilitating and dangerous medical symptoms exhibited by hospitalized persons. Advocates of this perspective view people who go to mental hospitals as *patients*. On the other side, advocates of the societal reaction approach have great doubts about the severity and the unambiguously medical nature of symptoms exhibited by hospitalized persons. From this perspective, people who go to mental hospitals are viewed as *deviants* because their "symptoms" are so varied and so subject to different interpretations.

The second key idea on which our patient typology is built is the kinds of social and economic resources people have available. For example, a married person is more likely to have supportive relationships than an unmarried person. An employed person is more likely to have economic resources and a better general standing in the community than a person not in the labor force or unemployed. A person with a high level of education may be better able to represent his or her interests through skills developed by education than a less well educated person. Persons who have resources that can be drawn upon in a time of crisis or trouble may be viewed as *protected*. Persons without such resources may be seen as *vulnerable*.

Thus, we were able to consider four types of patients, depending upon the kind of behavior that led to their hospitalization and the availability of social and economic resources. The types are:

Protected Patients: persons with resources who are committed for severe medical-psychiatric symptoms.
Vulnerable Patients: persons with few resources who are committed for severe medical-psychiatric symptoms.
Protected Deviants: persons with resources who are committed for nonmedical or nonpsychiatric symptoms.

Vulnerable Deviants: persons with few resources who are committed for nonmedical or nonpsychiatric symptoms.

We have examined the experiences of these four types at different stages in the career of the mental patient. Special attention was given to the characteristics of the social networks from which the patients came and to the role played by networks in the patient's career. Thus, we have been able to assess the relative importance of a patient's symptoms, resources, and social networks in influencing how hospitalization occurs, what happens after hospitalization, and whether a patient is released from the hospital.

Endnotes

1. H.G. Kaplan and G.J. Warheit, "Introduction to 'Recent Developments in the Sociology of Mental Illness,' " *Journal of Health and Social Behavior* 16 (December 1975):344.

2. For an example of the use of screening devices in household interviews, see J.K. Myers, J.J. Lindenthal, and M.P. Pepper, "Life Events, Social Integration, and Psychiatric Symptomatology," *Journal of Health and Social Behavior* 16 (December 1975):421–27.

3. L. Milazzo-Sayre, "Changes in the Age, Sex, and Diagnostic Composition of Admissions to State and County Mental Hospitals, United States 1969–1975," *Mental Health Statistical Note No. 148*, U.S. Department of Health, Education and Welfare (May 1978).

4. R.E.L. Faris and H.W. Dunham, *Mental Disorders in Urban Areas* (Chicago: University of Chicago Press, 1939).

5. See, for example, M.L. Kohn and J.A. Clausen, "Social Isolation and Schizophrenia," *American Sociological Review* 20 (April 1955):265–73; M.L. Kohn, "Class, Family, and Schizophrenia: A Reformulation," *Social Forces* 50 (March 1972):295–309; M.H. Brenner, *Mental Illness and the Economy* (Cambridge, Mass.: Harvard University Press, 1973); and W.R. Gove and J.F. Tudor, "Adult Sex Roles and Mental Illness," *American Journal of Sociology* 78 (January 1973):812–35.

6. Kohn, "Class, Family, and Schizophrenia."

7. W.A. Rushing and T. Ortega, "Socioeconomic Status and Mental Disorder: New Evidence and a Sociomedical Formulation," *American Journal of Sociology* 84 (March 1979):1175–1200.

8. Rushing and Ortega, "Socioeconomic Status," p. 1190.

9. W.R. Gove, "Societal Reaction as an Explanation of Mental Illness: An Evaluation," *American Sociological Review* 35 (December 1970):877.

10. Ibid., p. 879.

11. For discussion of these matters, see T.J. Scheff, "The Societal Reaction to Deviance: Ascriptive Elements in the Psychiatric Screening of Mental Patients

in a Midwestern State," *Social Problems* 11 (1964):401–13; T.J. Scheff, *Being Mentally Ill: A Sociological Theory* (Chicago: Aldine, 1966); and T.J. Scheff, "Schizophrenia as Ideology," *Schizophrenia Bulletin* 1 (Fall 1970):15–19.

12. See, for example, B. Dohrenwend, "Sociocultural and Social-Psychological Factors in the Genesis of Mental Disorders," *Journal of Health and Social Behavior* 16 (December 1975):365–92; and S. Worland and T. Weirath, "Validating the Langner Scale: A Critical Review," *Social Problems* 26 (December 1978):223–31.

13. E. Lemert, *Social Pathology* (New York: McGraw-Hill, 1951); H. Becker, *The Other Side: Perspectives on Deviance* (New York: Free Press, 1964).

14. Scheff, "Schizophrenia as Ideology," p. 17.

15. See, for example, Scheff, *Being Mentally Ill*; W.A. Rushing, "Individual Resources, Societal Reaction, and Hospital Commitment," *American Journal of Sociology* 77 (November 1971):511–26; W.A. Rushing, "Status Resources, Societal Reactions, and Mental Hospital Admission," *American Sociological Review* 43 (August 1978):521–33; and R. Perrucci, *Circle of Madness: On Being Insane and Institutionalized in America* (Englewood Cliffs, N.J.: Prentice-Hall, 1974).

16. For a discussion of these research findings, see Scheff, "The Societal Reaction to Deviance"; D.L. Wenger and C.R. Fletcher, "The Effect of Legal Counsel on Admissions to a State Mental Hospital: A Confrontation of Professions," *Journal of Health and Social Behavior* 10 (June 1969):66–72; Rushing, "Individual Resources"; J.R. Greenley, "The Psychiatric Patient's Family and the Length of Hospitalization," *Journal of Health and Social Behavior* 13 (March 1972):25–37; and R. Perrucci and S.D. Wallach, "Models of Mental Illness and Duration of Hospitalization," *Community Mental Health Journal* 13 (1975):271–79.

17. See Gove, "Societal Reaction as an Explanation of Mental Illness"; W.R. Gove, "Who Is Hospitalized: A Critical Review of Some Sociological Studies of Mental Illness," *Journal of Health and Social Behavior* 11 (December 1970):294–304; and W.R. Gove and P. Howell, "Individual Resources and Mental Hospitalization: A Comparison and Evaluation of the Societal Reaction and Psychiatric Perspectives," *American Sociological Review* 39 (February 1974):86–100.

18. T.J. Scheff, "The Labelling Theory of Mental Illness," *American Sociological Review* 39 (June 1974):444–52.

19. Rushing, "Status Resources"; W.A. Rushing and J. Esco, "Status Resources and Behavior Deviance as Contingencies of Societal Reaction," *Social Forces* 56 (September 1977):132–47.

20. The best theoretical discussion of the career of the mental patient is still to be found in E. Goffman, *Asylums* (Garden City, N.Y.: Doubleday, 1961). An excellent collection of readings built around a career perspective can be found in S.P. Spitzer and N.K. Denzin, eds., *The Mental Patient: Studies on the Sociology of Deviance* (New York: McGraw-Hill, 1968). A number of empirical studies have also focused on the factors involved in releasing persons from mental hospitals. See, for example, Greenley, "The Psychiatric Patient's Family"; Perrucci and Wallach, "Models of Mental Illness"; and W.R. Gove and T. Fain, "The Length of Psychiatric Hospitalization," *Social Problems* 22 (February 1975):407–19. For an examination of posthospital adjustment, see H.E.

Freeman and O.G. Simmons, "Mental Patients in the Community: Family Settings and Performance Levels," *American Sociological Review* 23 (April 1958):147–54; B. Pasamanick, F.R. Scarpitti, and S. Dinitz, *Schizophrenia in the Community: An Experimental Study in the Prevention of Hospitalization* (New York: Appleton-Century-Crofts, 1967); and S.S. Angrist, M. Lefton, S. Dinitz, and B. Pasamanick, *Women after Treatment: A Study of Former Mental Patients and Their Normal Neighbors* (New York: Appleton-Century-Crofts, 1968).

21. Examples of such research are found in J.A. Clausen, "The Impact of Mental Illness: A Twenty-Year Follow-up," in T.R. Wirt, G. Winokur, and M. Roff, eds., *Life History Research in Psychopathology* (Minneapolis: University of Minnesota Press, 1975), vol. IV; and C.L. Huffine and J.A. Clausen, "Madness and Work: Short- and Long-Term Effects of Mental Illness on Occupational Careers," *Social Forces* 57 (June 1979):1049–62.

22. W.A. Rushing, "Status Resources."

23. W.R. Gove and T. Fain, "A Comparison of Voluntary and Committed Psychiatric Patients," *Archives of General Psychiatry* 34 (1977):669–76.

24. For a discussion of these matters, see H.J. Steadman, "The Psychiatrist as a Conservative Agent of Social Control," *Social Problems* 20 (Fall 1972):263–71; J.R. Greenley, "Alternative Views of the Psychiatrist's Role," *Social Problems* 20 (Fall 1972):252–62; and H. Garfinkel, *Studies in Ethnomethodology* (Englewood Cliffs, N.J.: Prentice-Hall, 1968).

25. Rushing and Esco, in "Status Resources and Behavior Deviance," have noted that voluntary admissions may be subject to societal reactions similar to those experienced by nonvoluntary admissions.

26. W.C. Schwartz, Jr., and S. Dumpman, "Voluntary Commitment by Persuasion," *Hospital Community Psychiatry* 23 (April 1972):128–29.

27. J.R. Greenley, "Familial Expectations, Post-Hospital Adjustments, and Societal Reaction," *Journal of Health and Social Behavior* 20 (September 1979): 217–27.

28. R.J. Kleiner and S. Parker, "Network Participation and Psychosocial Impairment in an Urban Environment," in P. Meadows and E.H. Mizruchi, eds., *Urbanism, Urbanization, and Change* (Reading, Mass.: Addison-Wesley, 1976), pp. 322–36.

29. J.A. Clausen and M. Yarrow, eds., "The Impact of Mental Illness on the Family," *Journal of Social Issues* 11 (January 1955).

30. See, for example, M. Hammer, "Influence of Small Social Networks as Factors in Mental Hospital Admission," *Human Organization* 22 (1963–64):243–51; J.B. McKinlay, "Social Networks, Lay Consultation, and Help-Seeking Behavior," *Social Forces* 51 (March 1973):275–92; A. Horwitz, "Social Networks and Pathways to Psychiatric Treatment," *Social Forces* 56 (September 1977):36–105; and M. Pilisuk and C. Froland, "Kinship, Social Networks, Social Support and Health," *Social Science and Medicine* 120 (1978):273–80.

31. J.C. Mitchell, "The Concept and Use of Social Networks," in J.C. Mitchell, ed., *Social Networks in Urban Situations* (England: Manchester University Press, 1969); J. Boussevain and J.C. Mitchell, eds., *Network Analysis: Studies in Human Interaction* (The Hague: Mouton, 1973); N.E. Whitten and A.W. Wolfe, "Network Analysis," in J.J. Honigmann, ed., *Handbook of Social and*

Cultural Anthropology (Chicago: Rand McNally, 1973); and B. Anderson and M.L. Carlos, "What Is Social Network Theory?" in T. Burns and W. Buckley, eds., *Power and Control: Social Structures and Their Transformation* (Beverly Hills, Calif.: Sage, 1976).

32. Horwitz, "Social Networks."
33. Hammer, "Influence of Small Social Networks," p. 250.

Chapter 2

PATIENT TYPES
AND SOCIAL NETWORKS

Symptoms or resources—the debate continues over which is more crucial to an understanding of mental illness. So far neither approach has, by itself, been able to answer all the important questions. Meanwhile, the role of social networks in shaping the careers of mental patients has been all but ignored. We contend that symptoms *and* resources *and* social networks should be taken into account. Our analytic strategy includes the patient's illness, social vulnerability, and social network as important interacting factors in the patient's career.

The typology of patients and the social network approach were introduced in Chapter 1. In this chapter we discuss in more detail the way in which symptoms and resources were combined to produce the four patient types. We then elaborate on the meaning of symptoms and resources for social networks and for the career of the mental patient.

Building a Typology of Patients

The first step in building the typology was to group the forty-seven cases referred to in Chapter 1 according to the nature of the unusual behaviors for which persons were committed.[1] These behaviors may reflect psychiatric symptoms of a bizarre nature, or they may reflect symptoms that can be more easily explained in nonpsychiatric terms.

The information used to classify the committing symptoms was taken from the presenting data in the mental hospital records. Each researcher independently read the presenting data and classified the committing symptom(s) as primarily psychiatric or as primarily nonpsychiatric.[2] In some cases the classification of the presenting symptoms was clearly psychiatric, as in the following statements from the patient's wife and his physician:

CASE 232 [Question: Describe the behavior that leads you to believe that this person is mentally ill.]

Wife: He believes I'm being blackmailed; he believes I'm a tramp; he believes people are stealing his money.

Physician: Patient is psychotic, schizophrenic. Believes himself to be the Lord, connected with the Secret Service. Says he has invented a machine that other governments want and he needs protection from the police. Well-developed delusional system.

In other cases the classification of the presenting data was nonpsychiatric. The following lengthy entry from presenting data, in addition to containing nonpsychiatric data, includes the staff conclusion that the patient is experiencing a "marital problem":

CASE 240 The patient's daughter reported to me that she began getting depressed after she was fired from a job last year. The patient refused to look for another job, claiming that she had no self-confidence. She then began to refuse to do her household chores. She insisted that her husband buy her a new washing machine, and yet when he did she refused to use it. She also could not stand noise and refused to answer the phone, saying she was afraid of it. We asked the patient if she ever thought of killing herself, and she said she had. However, she also said that she did not think she would and did not consider the idea seriously.

In this case both the team and the family agreed that the problem was largely a marital problem. However, because there are no community resources around ———— County and because this person has been to [this hospital] for a preadmission study previously, we felt that we should admit the patient. We therefore agreed to admit her for short-term hospitalization, hoping to help her adjust better to her home situation.

Not all the presenting data was so clear as to the psychiatric or nonpsychiatric content of the patient's behavior. Therefore, after having read and classified the cases independently, we compared our judgements. In cases where our classifications did not match, we discussed the rationale for both the medical-psychiatric and the societal reaction interpretations until we reached a consensus. As a result of this analysis, we classified twenty-four individuals as *patients* and twenty-three as *deviants*.

Availability of social and economic resources was the second basis for grouping the forty-seven patients. The information on social and economic resources—that is, whether patients were married, employed, or had at least a high school education—was taken from the hospital records. If we had considered single resources, we could have categorized the patients in various ways. For example, eleven patients were married, twenty-three had high school diplomas, and twelve were employed. However, we contend that the importance of these resources lies in the whole picture they form—that is, of an individual who possesses adequate or inadequate, many or few resources. Therefore, we constructed a measure of overall status resources for each patient. Patients were viewed as possessing one resource for each of the following characteristics: married, graduated from high school, and employed immediately prior to hospitalization. Patients with two or three of these characteristics we considered as having high resources—that is, as *protected*. Fourteen patients were protected; three were married and had high school diplomas, seven had high school diplomas and were employed, and three were married and employed. Only one patient possessed all three characteristics. We viewed patients with none or one of the characteristics as *vulnerable*. Thirty-three patients were included in this category; sixteen possessed no resources, and of those who possessed single attributes, four were married, twelve had high school diplomas, and one was employed.

We then cross-classified resources and symptoms to produce four groups of patients: fourteen Vulnerable Patients, nineteen Vulnerable Deviants, ten Protected Patients, and four Protected Deviants. The ways in which single and combined resources were distributed among patient types is displayed in Table 2.1.

Symptoms, Resources, and Networks

Grouping of patients into four types based on committing symptoms and on resources is designed to facilitate analysis. However, the committing symptoms should not be interpreted as the only evidence of the nature of patients' problems. It is our contention that the committing symptoms have been selected by a social network from a wider range of symptoms. Social networks see their troubled

Table 2.1 Patient Types and Distribution of Status Resources

	I Vulnerable Patients (14)	II Vulnerable Deviants (19)	III Protected Patients (10)	IV Protected Deviants (4)
No resources	6	10	0	0
Married	2	2	6	1
High school diploma	6	6	7	4
Employed	0	1	8	3
Married/diploma	0	0	2	1
Diploma/employed	0	0	4	3
Married/employed	0	0	3	0

network member exhibit a variety of unusual behaviors over a longer or shorter period of time. When individuals think about these behaviors or discuss them with others, they tend to narrow down the number of problem behaviors and focus upon only a few. This selection makes discussion easier and allows network members to have common understandings about the problems they are experiencing. The result is that social networks move beyond the broader set of unusual behaviors to focus upon a smaller number of problem behaviors of special concern.

To illustrate this process we must turn our attention to the initial unusual behaviors that set in motion the chain of events that results in hospitalization. We look first at all the initial unusual behaviors reported by all network members to see whether the problematic behaviors exhibited by pre-patients are clearly indicative of mental illness or whether the behaviors suggest acts of deviance explainable in other than psychiatric terms. Next we look at consensus and variation within networks concerning the reported content of the unusual behaviors.

In order to examine the initial unusual behaviors that eventually resulted in hospitalization, all network members (family, friends, and acquaintances of the forty-seven patients) were asked to describe when they *first noticed* anything unusual in the patient's behavior. Our interest was in specific events or in things the patient may have done or said that made people take notice and raise questions. Network members were asked to recall the incident in which the *first suspicious behavior* they had observed occurred. If an incident had produced more than one behavior, we asked network members to select the first behavior that prompted them to question the pre-patient's general behavior.

When network members described the first time they had noticed anything unusual about a patient's behavior, they indicated quite a bit of variability in symptom content. Symptoms cited included both those that fit the medical-psychiatric model and those indicative of problems with everyday living (Table 2.2 contains a classification of all the first unusual behaviors observed by network members according to general symptom categories). Symptoms included delusions and hallucinations, strange and annoying habits or bizarre behavior, social withdrawal, strange facial expressions, physical complaints, assaultive or aggressive behavior, failures in role behavior, and violation of codes of decency.

The behaviors reported most frequently by network members were physical complaints, followed closely by delusions and hallucinations and by strange or annoying habits or bizarre behavior. Much less frequent mention was made of behavior classified as strange facial expressions and as violations of codes of decency.

Does this variation occur only across networks and lead to the differences in committal symptoms? When we look at the consensus among all members of a social network on initial symptoms, we find that 42 percent of the networks had at least a majority consensus about the first behavior observed. Twenty-one percent had a complete consensus. However, in 57 percent of the networks, there was agreement among 50 percent or less of the network members as to the first problematic behavior.

A look at some case materials provides examples of networks in which there was a consensus and networks in which none existed. In the first case, statements from five network members seem to agree

Table 2.2   First Unusual Behavior Observed by Network Members

Unusual Behavior	Number	Percentage
Physical complaints	41	20.6
Delusions and hallucinations	36	18.1
Strange and annoying habits or bizarre behavior	31	15.6
Failures in role behavior	21	10.6
Assaultive or aggressive behavior	20	10.1
Social withdrawal	14	7.0
Strange facial expressions	5	2.5
Violation of codes of decency	4	2.0
No answer	27	13.6
Total	199	100.1

in terms of the general description of the unusual behavior that prompted concern. Note that even when there is a general consensus about behavior, there is room for focusing on different aspects of the behavior:

CASE 230-01   *Father:* The second day he was home we both went out to clean the garage out and he just blew up real fast. He really blew up. He didn't make any sense and the things he said were muddled.

CASE 230-02   *Mother:* When he came home from the service (in March) . . . his personality was different. He was very hostile and rebellious. He was very irrational at times; you just couldn't understand him. He didn't make sense in his speech. He'd ramble on and we couldn't understand him. He had temper tantrums, and it just wasn't him.

CASE 230-03   *Grandmother:* When he came home from the army we went over to dinner and he walked in. Of course I got up and kissed him, and he sat down and ate his supper and got right up and left. I told his grandpa when we left that there was something radically wrong with him. And he looked terrible. That was in March.

CASE 230-05   *Aunt:* Around Thanksgiving of 1969 he seemed like he was in another world. He wasn't talkative. Someone asked him to say a prayer at the table and he refused. He would talk to himself.

CASE 230-06   *Uncle:* The first time I noticed any change at all in Robert was when he was discharged from the service. He has probably been out of the service maybe three to four months now, maybe longer. He was discharged in April or May. I lose track of the time because I keep so busy and occupied with things that I lose track of time. When Robert came home from the service, we had a family get-together and we used to try to sit down and visit with Bob like we used to, reminisce. He would get up, go out of the room, not say a word, go out and go to his bedroom. Here we had all come to see Bob, not his mother and father, my brother or sister-in-law, we had come to see Bob, and Bob picks himself up and goes, leaves, or he would jump into his car and take off. And here we had come up to see him. This is not like Bob. Bob likes to talk and reminisce as well as anybody, and he said nothing. You want to start a conversation, to talk his "shop," what he just came from, the Navy. Well, "How's the Navy, Bob?" or this and that or the other, food, and so on. He said nothing, he didn't discuss the service at all. Correction, Bob was in the Army, his brother was in the Navy. He was in a motor pool and we heard he was driving a jeep for this CO. I thought this was a fine job for him. Then I heard he was a mechanic and I thought this was great, he could use that when he came out. Nothing, he didn't discuss nothing, he didn't want to talk about nothing. Matter of fact, he scarcely said hello. So this is when I noticed that this was not the Bob that I know.

The sixth network member describes altogether different behavior and at a much earlier time:

CASE 230-08 *Uncle:* I seen when he was in junior high school that he started going the other way . . . away from his family. He started going in the opposite way than his family. He started dope then . . . started smoking marijuana and running around with the wrong crowd. He didn't care how he looked or dressed.

In the following case, three of four network members report problems that center on job difficulties:

CASE 428-01 *Husband:* Four years ago. It was her first time working at any employment, and at the time I didn't realize what this was leading up to. She would come home crying about her job. I mean she didn't claim that people were picking on her but she wasn't used to people working together and all the bickering that goes on when you get a group together. It upset her quite a bit. She would get into quite lengthy crying spells at times, and that was my first indication. But as I say, at the time I didn't realize that it was leading up to this.

CASE 428-02 *Mother-in-law:* I don't know . . . as I said, she was always so good to me and I suppose that's why it hurts so bad. It's been about a year and a half. She took me to town because I do not drive, and I asked her to take me to the neighbor's to take a dish of food over there, and I say something to her and she bit me off . . . kind of cross . . . and I don't think I had ever heard Pauline speak a cross word to me. So that was just so out of the ordinary. Then another time that she took me she just didn't talk. You could talk but she wouldn't answer you. Maybe it wasn't the best policy, but I thought that if I talked to her or called, I would only cross her so I'm just going to stand by . . . if there's anything I can do, I'll do it.

CASE 428-03 *Father:* I think about the time they bought the farm they live on and she decided . . . or somebody made the decision, I don't know who . . . that she would go to work and try to help out a little bit. She went to help cook at the high school. That was about three or four years ago, I guess. I think she done awful good to start with and then they went, trying to put her at the cash register and then that kind of upset her. She didn't think that she could handle the change and they kind of insisted and I think that's what kind of throwed her off too. That's just my opinion. I think that's what she told her mother . . . that she just didn't think she could do that job.

CASE 428-04 *Mother:* It's been quite a while. The first of it was when she started to work at the school building—she was cooking. Every night she'd call me and say she'd have to talk to me every night in the world. Now I don't know what happened there but that was the start of it. She would talk about different things but wouldn't get to the cause, and I wondered why. Then after she was working there awhile they asked her to take care of the money, and she called me about that and said she knew she couldn't do it. I told her it would actually be much easier for her to do that and that sometimes by thinking you can't, and you try it is much easier than you ever think it will be. But she said she couldn't and didn't want to try. That's been about three–four years now.

In the following case, reports from different network members vary as to the content of the first unusual behavior. Some reports contain medical referents such as hallucinations; others indicate problems of everyday living such as trouble in school:

CASE 408-01   *Mother:* It could have started in high school, he wasn't studying, failing his grades. When I got married he was very disappointed. He wasn't happy, he didn't want me to get married until he graduated from high school. After I got married we quarreled, I wanted him to come to G——— with me and my husband, and he wanted to stay in T——— because of school. He'd laugh and talk to himself. He'd lie in bed and look at the ceiling instead of doing his lessons.

CASE 408-02   *Grandmother:* The first time was when he had trouble with school, he had some kind of sickness and he didn't go to school. Then when he went back to school he couldn't make up everything. It happened when he was sixteen. He was sick. He was in the hospital a couple of days, he had the runoff—you know what I mean, the bowels. When his father died, he fell on the floor (about six years ago).

CASE 408-03   *Uncle:* About 4½ years ago. He told me that he saw flying saucers.

CASE 408-04   *Aunt:* When ——— was finishing the room at ——— after [patient's] father died. He wanted to do something and he would do it. We knew then and there that there was something wrong with him. We thought it was because of his father's death. (That was August or September of 1964). He wanted to do something. They were laying flooring and he wanted to lay the subflooring and nail it down, he wouldn't do it. ——— waited for him to do it, but this went on through the whole room. He said he would do it tomorrow.

CASE 408-05   *Aunt:* He kept repeating things all the time, that was about a year ago.

CASE 408-06   *Aunt:* About four or five years ago, he would sit on a chair and wink and throw kisses.

CASE 408-07   *Friend of patient:* It really surprised me when he said he was going to see a psychiatrist. One thing that was bad was that he struck his mother. He'd tell me what he was doing with his stepfather—

arguments and sometimes almost going to blows. He'd dwell on his problems—I noticed that quite a bit about him—about his problems in school and what he wanted to do with his future. He wanted to go to college. He'd yell at his mother and tell her that she didn't know what she was talking about—and his sister and his brother-in-law.

As these case materials indicate, patients exhibit numerous symptoms, some of which can be normalized or explained in everyday terms, and some of which are so bizarre as to be amenable only to a medical-psychiatric explanation. Faced with numerous symptoms, networks can focus on those that are more problematic for the network or that fit the network's definition and understanding of mental illness. For example, networks whose members have more education are likely to focus on behaviors that reflect a standard definition of the symptoms of mental illness.

Within our framework, symptom selection is important not only to the committal process; it will affect the entire career of the patient. We expect that the symptoms networks focus on in committing a patient will be significant factors in influencing expectations among network members about hospital experiences. The medical model of mental illness defines the mental hospital as a source of treatment and cure. The choice of medical-psychiatric symptoms indicates that the network expects the patient to recover and leave the hospital. Conversely, a focus on everyday problems may indicate that a network realizes it cannot control the pre-patient and therefore expects that the hospital will do so. Social control—in contrast to cure—implies lengthy, if not permanent, hospitalization.

The career of the mental patient should be related not only to symptoms but also to the way in which resources affect the expectations of network members regarding their future with the patient. Resources of a pre-patient may be used by the network as an index of whether the patient will recover and be self-sufficient. Employment, for example, reflects current income, contact with people outside the family, and future ability to hold down a job. Education represents an achieved status as well as a skill level that has implications for future employment opportunities. Marriage is evidence of involvement with another person and indicates that a patient has a home after release.

Neither the symptom choices nor the resources occur in isolation. Taken together, they form a picture of the patient—a picture the network has helped to create but to which the network also reacts. Symptoms chosen by the networks and the status resources available to the patient should influence the prediction the network makes about recovery. In turn, expectations about recovery should influence the degree of continued contact between the patient and the network. Finally, paths to the mental hospital should be related to the likelihood of leaving the hospital.

The strategy of studying symptoms, resources, and social networks should enable us to better understand the career of the mental patient from the initial unusual behavior through release from the hospital. In addition, we should be able to better identify, and perhaps reconcile, some of the points of difference between the two competing perspectives on mental illness that have dominated much of our theory and research. Thus, we may be able to move beyond the old perspectives to an alternative formulation that sheds greater light on the career of a mental patient.

Endnotes

1. See Appendix C for a description of the research design.
2. Our purpose was not to make a medical or psychiatric judgement of the symptoms as might be done in a clinical setting by a trained professional. We attempted to classify the behaviors exhibited solely in response to their manifest content, which is the way network members are most likely to respond. Medical-psychiatric symptoms are those of an extremely bizarre, unusual, or serious nature for which there is no conventional explanation. Non–medical-psychiatric symptoms are those that may have a conventional referent or a normalizing component.

Chapter 3

NETWORK STRUCTURE AND REACTIONS TO INITIAL UNUSUAL BEHAVIOR

The career of a mental patient begins with the first occasion on which some behavior he or she exhibits is judged by other persons as sufficiently different, unusual, or problematic to be noteworthy. In Chapter 2 we examined unusual behaviors, or acts of *primary deviation,* which we found to be quite varied, covering a wide array of circumstances and involving different degrees of apparent severity and risk.

For initial unusual behaviors to be considered acts of primary deviation, they must be exhibited in a social context and must elicit a reaction from persons who observe or learn about the behavior. Reactions to initial unusual behaviors can be influenced by the nature of the acts observed, by characteristics of the actor, and by characteristics of the observer. Acts of an extremely bizarre or serious nature may be the sole determinant of how people react and may constitute *prima facie* evidence of illness. A person's characteristics—for example, a questionable moral character or a reputation for strange activities—may also determine how other persons react to initial unusual behavior. Reactions may also be influenced by the characteristics of the social network in which the actor and the observer are involved. For example, observers with exceptional knowledge of psychological problems may be especially sensitive to behaviors that less trained observers might ignore.

In this chapter we turn our attention to the social network in which the pre-patient is embedded and in which the initial unusual behaviors are exhibited. The *social network* is defined as all those persons who had social relationships with the pre-patient in the months preceding hospitalization or who were involved in the hospitalization decision. Our purposes are: (1) to describe the composition and structure of the social networks in which patients are involved, (2) to determine what relationship, if any, exists between the characteristics of social networks and their reaction to initial unusual behaviors, and (3) to examine the uniformity or variability of reactions across the four groups into which we have classified patients.

Composition and Structure of Social Networks

As mentioned earlier, we have focused attention on forty-seven social networks, each of which decided to hospitalize one of its members for mental illness. The networks had a total of 321 members (excluding the 47 patients), for an average size of 6.8 persons per network. The networks were composed primarily of family members; about one fifth of the network members were nonfamily persons such as friends, co-workers, and community professionals (see Table 3.1). The persons most directly involved with patients prior to commitment were members of the immediate families, and other relatives.

The four patient types showed some differences in the composition of their social networks (see Table 3.2). The mean size of social

Table 3.1   Composition of Social Networks

Relationship to Patient	Number	Percentage of Total Network
Mother	29	9.0
Father	21	6.6
Spouse	12	3.8
Sibling	54	16.9
Child (over 16)	11	3.4
Child (under 16)	49	15.3
Other relative	82	25.6
Employer or co-worker	9	2.8
Community professional	7	2.2
Neighbor or friend	46	14.4
Total	320	100.0

Table 3.2 Patient Types and Composition of Social Networks

Relationship to Patient	Vulnerable Patients (14)		Vulnerable Deviants (19)		Protected Patients (10)		Protected Deviants (4)	
	Number	Percentage	Number	Percentage	Number	Percentage	Number	Percentage
Parent	18	20.0	18	15.9	10	11.5	4	14.3
Spouse	2	2.2	3	2.6	7	6.9	1	3.6
Sibling	17	18.5	19	16.8	14	16.1	4	14.3
Child	17	18.5	16	14.2	18	20.7	9	32.1
Other relative	24	26.0	38	33.6	12	13.8	8	28.6
Neighbor or friend	12	13.0	12	10.6	20	23.0	2	7.4
Employer or co-worker	2	2.0	3	2.6	4	4.6	0	—
Community professional	0	—	4	3.5	3	3.4	0	—
Total	92		113		88		28	
Mean network size	6.6		5.9		8.8		7.0	
Mean nonfamily members	1.0		1.0		2.7		0.5	
Mean children under 16	1.1		0.5		1.5		2.2	
Mean children under 16 for patients with children	2.5(6)		2.0(5)		3.0(5)		3.0(3)	
Marital status								
Single	7		11		3		1	
Married	2		3		7		1	
Divorced	5		4		0		2	
Widowed	0		1		0		0	
Sex								
Male	5		6		6		1	
Female	9		13		4		3	
Median age	32		32		42		30	

networks was smaller for Vulnerable Patients and Vulnerable Deviants, both of which groups contained patients characterized by few social resources. The largest networks were for Protected Patients—that is, patients with medical symptoms and with many social resources. Protected Patients also had considerably more nonfamily members in their social networks than did the other patient types.

There were some differences in the pattern of dependent children across patient types. Both Protected Patients and Protected Deviants were more likely to have dependent children, and they had a larger number of them (3.0) than did either of the other patient types. This finding is to be expected because one of the resources these patients can have is being married, which increases the likelihood of their having children.

In general, the composition of the social networks out of which the patients came seems rather conventional; the networks contained parents, siblings, relatives, friends, and children. Patients were not social isolates—at least not these particular first admissions to a mental hospital. However, one aspect of the composition of social networks that may not have been too conventional was the marital and sexual status of the patients. Slightly more than half (twenty-five of forty-seven) of the patients had ever been married, and almost half of those ever married had been divorced. (These divorces took place prior to hospitalization). Of the eleven divorced patients, ten were female. In addition, more than three out of five of the first admissions were female.

It is worth noting that among Protected Patients were found the largest proportion of married persons (with no divorces) and the largest proportion of males. Protected Patients were also considerably older than other patients; their average age was forty-two—that is, ten to twelve years senior to other patients.

What about the structure of these social networks? What was the nature of the emotional ties among members of the networks? How frequently did network members interact with the patient? Did some networks have a clear structure of leadership? The following sections consider some aspects of the structure of social networks.

Density of Ties

The average size of social networks ranged from a low of 5.9 members (Vulnerable Deviants) to a high of 8.7 members (Protected

Patients). The larger the network, the greater the number of possible ties that can exist among members. Our estimate of the density of ties in a network was based on the reported frequency of interaction among network members. A scoring system was used that assigned a value of four when network members reported daily contact with each other, a value of three for weekly contact, and a value of two for monthly contact. Protected Patients' networks had the highest average contact score (3.6), which indicated almost daily contact among members. Networks of Vulnerable Patients had the lowest contact score (1.6), which indicated that members saw each other only about once a month.

Openness

A patient's social network can be composed of a small circle of close relatives, with little or no contact with "outsiders," or it can be open in the sense that nonfamily members have interaction with the patient and other network members. As was noted in Table 3.1, only about one fifth of all network members were unrelated to patients. However, this overall figure does not tell us how many of the social networks were closed and how many were open.

Among Vulnerable Patients, eight of the fourteen networks were composed exclusively of family members. Vulnerable Deviants' networks were also somewhat closed to outsiders (ten of nineteen networks were exclusively family members), while three of the four networks of Protected Deviants were closed. Only the networks of Protected Patients were open networks in the sense that almost all of them had ties with nonfamily members.

Ties to Patient

All network members were asked to identify the one person closest to the patient in terms of emotional bonds, helping relations, and confidence. Many persons in each network could name at least one person whom they believed to have a close, emotional tie with the patient. Our concern was not whether anyone was named as close, but the degree of consensus a social network exhibited in the selection of "significant others" for a patient. If half or more of the network members named the same person as having close ties to the patient, we considered it a "majority consensus." If at least two persons, but less than half the network members, mentioned the same person as close to a patient, we considered it a "minority consensus." When the same person was not nominated more than once as being close to a patient, we classified that network as having no one with a close emotional tie to the patient.

Overall, twenty-one of the forty-seven networks had a majority consensus in naming someone who had close ties with the patient; seven of forty-seven had a minority consensus on a significant other; and nineteen of forty-seven networks had no one with close ties to the patient. The pattern of close ties with the patient across the different patient categories showed some variability. There was a majority consensus on the existence of a "significant other" in about 33 percent of the Vulnerable Patient networks, 40 percent of the Vulnerable Deviant networks, 50 percent of the Protected Patient networks, and 25 percent of the Protected Deviant networks. Considering both majority and minority consensus on the existence of a "significant other," almost all Protected Patient networks had someone with close ties to the patient. Two thirds of Vulnerable Deviant networks and half of Vulnerable Patient networks had a significant other for the patient when minority consensus was considered. Networks without a significant other close to the patient were more abundant among Vulnerable Patients, followed by Vulnerable Deviants, Protected Deviants, and Protected Patients. Only 10 percent of the Protected Patient networks were without a member close to the patient.

Ties among Members

Each network member was asked to describe the nature of the ties that existed among all network members. Respondents were asked to provide a general assessment ranging from "very close" to "not close at all." As with the previous structural characteristics, we aggregated the responses of individual network members to obtain the majority view for the entire social network.

Among Vulnerable Patient and Vulnerable Deviant networks, there was an almost equal division of "close" and "not close" networks. Six of fourteen Vulnerable Patient networks had a majority of members who said the network was "close," and five of fourteen described their networks as "not close." Among Vulnerable Deviant networks, seven of nineteen were described as "close," and seven of nineteen as "not close" (the remaining five networks gave descriptions that were supported by a minority of members). Among Protected Deviant networks, three of four were described as "not close." Finally, among Protected Patient networks, eight of ten were described as "close."

Leadership

An effort was made to determine whether social networks contained persons viewed as leaders who could shape opinions and solve problems facing the network. Interest in leadership as a structural characteristic was based on the expectation that networks with key members would make decisions about the hospitalization of one of their members in a different way than would networks without leaders. All network members were asked: "Of all the people you have named who know the patient, which one would you say is most like a leader, most likely to be looked to by the others to make decisions or solve problems?"

Only eighteen of the forty-seven networks (38 percent) had a person for whom there was a majority consensus on his or her role as a leader. The largest proportion of networks with a majority consensus (60 percent) was found among Protected Patient networks. About 33 percent of the Vulnerable Patient and Vulnerable Deviant networks had a majority consensus. None of the networks for Protected Deviants had such a consensus.

Decision Making

Compared to developing a consensus on leadership, a larger proportion of social networks could develop a majority consensus on the existence of one person likely to make the important decisions facing the network. Twenty-six of forty-seven networks (55 percent) identified a decisionmaker, whereas only 38 percent identified a network leader. Greater certainty in the selection of decisionmakers seems due to a tendency automatically to choose persons in traditionally defined family roles (e.g., father, husband) as key decisionmakers. On the other hand, selection of a network leader (an opinion leader and problem solver) did not seem so susceptible to automatic choice of patriarchal roles.

Protected Patient networks again showed the greatest proportion (70 percent) of majority consensus in identifying a single network member as a decisionmaker. Fifty-eight percent of Vulnerable Deviant networks and 50 percent of Protected Deviant networks had a

Table 3.3 Summary of Structural Characteristics of Social Networks

Structural Characteristics	Vulnerable Patients	Vulnerable Deviants	Protected Patients	Protected Deviants
Density of ties	Medium density	Low density	High density	Medium density
Openness	Low–moderately open to nonfamily	Moderately open to nonfamily	Most open to nonfamily	Least open to nonfamily
Ties to patient	Close ties, few networks	Close ties, many networks	Close ties, almost all networks	Close ties, very few networks
Ties among members	About two of five networks with close ties	About one of three networks with close ties	Eight of ten networks with close ties	One of four networks with close ties
Leadership	Leader identified in 36% of networks	Leader identified in 37% of networks	Leader identified in 60% of networks	No leader identified in any network
Decision making	43% of networks with a decisionmaker	58% of networks with a decisionmaker	70% of networks with a decisionmaker	50% of networks with a decisionmaker

majority consensus on a decisionmaker. Vulnerable Patient networks had the smallest proportion (43 percent) of networks with a majority consensus on a decisionmaker.

Summary of Structural Characteristics

Table 3.3 contains a summary of the structural characteristics of social networks. A number of clear patterns can be observed. Social networks of Protected Patients were distinctly different: They had the largest number of members; they were most open to nonfamily members who had relationships with patients; almost all had at least one person recognized as having close ties with the patient; almost all networks were described by a majority of their members as having close ties among members; they had the largest proportion of networks with a consensus on the existence of a network leader and a network decisionmaker. In short, Protected Patient networks had close social-emotional ties among members (including the patient), and they were internally structured so as to achieve instrumental ends when confronted with a problem or with the need to make important decisions.

Differences among networks in the other three patient types were less pronounced. All three revealed a pattern of fewer networks with strong social-emotional bonds and an instrumental structure of leadership. Networks of Protected Deviants were especially weak in both social-emotional and instrumental structures. Such networks, in comparison to those of Protected Patients, would probably be less supportive of their patient members and less able to use their resources to assist their members.

Initial Unusual Behaviors

All network members were asked to describe the first time they had observed any unusual behaviors exhibited by the pre-patient. These unusual behaviors may or may not have been the same ones that later became the basis for hospitalization. In some cases, initial unusual behaviors preceded the hospitalization decision by fifteen years, while in other cases hospitalization took place several months after the problematic behavior was observed.

Of special concern was the nature of the initial unusual behaviors, when they occurred, how they were viewed by network members, and what actions were taken in response. Similarities or differences among any of these matters across the four patient categories may give us some clues as to the beginning of the career of a mental patient and may aid us in examining the competing theoretical views discussed in Chapter 1. Do the initial unusual behaviors prompt quick judgements about the existence of a serious mental illness, or do network members try to "explain away" the behavior or deny its seriousness? Are persons with few social resources more quickly judged as mentally ill and in need of hospitalization? Why are some networks able to sustain a member with problematic behavior for many years before hospitalization, while other networks move more quickly to hospitalize?

Our focus is not so much on the psychiatric or clinical content of the initial unusual behaviors as on the time of their occurrence and on their social content—that is, the way the behaviors are described by network members and their interpretation of the meaning and importance of the behaviors.

Time of Occurrence

Network members reported the observation of unusual behaviors for as short a time as one month prior to hospitalization ("When she came down here for a visit last month, she stared at me as if I was from outer space or something") or for as long as thirty-five years ("She has been peculiar all of her life, since about five years old"). Overall, thirteen of the forty-seven networks reported having observed the initial unusual behaviors within the year prior to hospitalization. Another fourteen networks made their observations from one to three years before hospitalization occurred. Eleven networks identified unusual behaviors for more long-standing periods ranging from four to forty years; most (nine of eleven), however, reported in the range of four to ten years. The remaining eight networks did not have any consensus among members as to when the initial unusual behaviors took place.

Comparison across the four patient categories indicates that the time elapsed between initial unusual behaviors and hospitalization was shortest among Protected Patients. Five of the ten Protected Patient networks reported initial unusual behaviors within the year prior to hospitalization, and another three networks identified unusual behaviors within three years prior to hospitalization. Among Vulnerable Patients, three of fourteen networks identified problem behavior in the year prior to hospitalization, and another four networks observed such behaviors within three years before hospitalization. Four of nineteen Vulnerable Deviant networks stated that the first unusual behavior occurred in the year before hospitalization, and six networks reported such behavior in the three years prior to hospitalization.

The interesting contrast is between the two "pure" types: Protected Patients had more social resources and were committed for apparently clear medical reasons; Vulnerable Deviants lacked social resources and were hospitalized for ambiguous or unclear medical reasons. Societal reaction theory, as discussed in Chapter 1, would predict that hospitalization would occur with greatest swiftness for persons with limited social resources. The data reported here, however, do not support this prediction; the patients with greatest resources exhibited the shortest lapse of time between initial unusual behavior and hospitalization. The data are also consistent with the views of Gove and Howell, who suggest that persons with more social and economic resources are more likely to seek out psychiatric help when they experience problems.[1] This finding may be due to the fact that persons with greater resources, as well as their social networks, have more knowledge of psychiatric treatment sources or less susceptibility to prejudicial beliefs about psychological disorders.

Description of and Reaction to Initial Unusual Behaviors

Given the rather substantial variation in the time elapsed between initial unusual behavior and hospitalization, we should examine the particular descriptions of behavior provided by network members. Some descriptions may appear to reflect clinical symptoms—an indication of the diffusion of psychiatric terminology among a lay public. Other descriptions may reflect the everyday language of people who try to cope with the problems they describe.

The nature of network members' descriptions of problem behavior may help us understand why some networks seem to act quickly and decisively to deal with the problems of one of their members, while other networks disagree over what may have occurred or the seriousness of the incident and vacillate over whether any action should be taken.

We begin with a comparison of the initial unusual behaviors of the two "pure" types (Vulnerable Deviants and Protected Patients). We already know these types differ on the nature of the problem behaviors (i.e., "symptoms") that resulted in hospitalization, since the differences provided one of the bases for the creation of the four patient types. However, we now consider initial unusual behaviors that occurred some time prior to hospitalization and in many cases resulted in no action or in undue concern by network members. In short, what we now present regarding initial unusual behaviors is not simply an artifact of the way we created our patient types. Any similarity could be due to a relationship between the initial unusual behaviors and the behaviors that ultimately led to a decision to hospitalize.

Vulnerable Deviant Patterns. The initial unusual behaviors noted by members of Vulnerable Deviant networks are couched in everyday language and thereby provide a veneer of normality for the behavior without implying that it is usual or desirable. One can live for many years in a very unpleasant family situation without describing the behavior of people responsible for the unpleasantness in either medical or psychiatric terms. In the following excerpts from interviews we try to demonstrate that the descriptions of initial unusual behaviors provided by network members deal with events, incidents, and relationships that may take place on a routine, day-to-day basis among persons who have already established identities and role relationships.

The first set of descriptions of initial unusual behaviors concerns reports of general change in role performance or personal grooming:

CASE 219 [38-year-old, white, unmarried male] It was a general reluctance to do things. We would tell him things to do with chores. He would get mad and resentful of me telling him about the chores.

CASE 203 [18-year-old, white, unmarried female] The only thing that I did notice when she was in the last six months of her high school, she would begin to be careless about herself, which she wasn't before. 'Cause that girl, as far as clothes, she never wanted nothing but the best. She'd go to the My Lady Shop, the Francis Shop, nothing but the best. In fact, I even had to close the account at the end, 'cause whether she needed it or not, she thought she needed or wanted a skirt and sweater, nothing but the best. And then the last six months I noticed, like I said, that she was getting more careless about herself.

CASE 227 [24-year-old, white, divorced female with three children] After she got married in September of 1965, she didn't fix her hair and never dressed. She ate a lot of fattening foods. She'd get up and eat a huge dish of ice cream for breakfast. I kept telling her that she shouldn't let herself go so soon because they were just married. Then in November, I had to go have an operation and I had no one working at the store. So my husband had Linda do it and she stole a bunch of things from the store. The next thing I noticed about her was the first New Year's Eve they spent together. I was home and my husband was home and Linda and Jack were going out. And she put on an old house dress that wasn't ironed, she didn't comb her hair, or put any makeup on and she just looked like a regular slob. And I said "Linda, don't tell me you're going out on New Year's Eve dressed like that." She said, "Oh it's dark, nobody is going to see us anyway." And I said, "Well your husband is going to see you," and she said, "Well it doesn't make any difference if he's here or not."

CASE 413 [22-year-old, white, married female with two children] I'd say when her mother was first put in the hospital, about two years ago. She was upset. When she found out that her mother had cancer she just changed. She was just nervous and upset and almost everything she done upset her. It was just her behavior. We'd just sit around and talk. Sometimes she'd come over and she'd be here for something like a few minutes and then she'd have to get up and go. She just never sit still very long; you know what I mean?

The network reactions to these four cases indicate either that the initial unusual behaviors were not taken seriously or that the network was divided in its judgement on the seriousness of the behaviors. In Case 219, one network member said, "I thought it was serious," while the other stated, "I didn't think it was serious enough to do anything about." In Case 227, three members of the network were firm in their view that the initial unusual behaviors were serious, while the other three were not so sure. The latter three stated: (1) "I didn't take it seriously because I thought she was just a kid and she hasn't grown up yet. I just didn't pay too much attention to her"; (2) "I didn't think it should be taken seriously"; and (3) "I thought it was serious when she got pregnant with the first baby. She had Dr. Smith as her doctor and he was also my doctor and he told me that Linda shouldn't have any more children because she didn't have the mentality to take care of them and that however many children she had I would have to raise them and I wasn't up for raising a lot of children." (We might interpret this last comment as serious, but not in a medical or psychological sense; it simply meant a serious problem for the respondent, who might have to raise the children.) In Case 413, four of five network members stated that the initial unusual behaviors were not serious. A typical statement was: "At the time I didn't think it was too serious. You know, everybody has problems. I just thought it would pass." Finally, in Case 203 the patient's mother was unable to make any judgement about the seriousness of the behaviors she had observed: "As far as her behavior, I really didn't know what to say. I know her behavior, as far as she wanting to sleep all the time, and of course her mouth was getting so . . . her language was getting something terrible, too. And when she'd show her temper she'd just curse something terrible. And she didn't care who she talked to. Let's say she just lost respect for everyone. She talked to me or a dog the same way. She didn't care how she talked to me."

Another set of descriptions of initial unusual behaviors among Vulnerable Deviants involves problems with legal authorities that can be viewed in a nonmedical perspective:

CASE 225 [34-year-old, white, unmarried male] About six or seven years ago when I think he robbed a store and a police car. They thought somebody down here robbed the store and they thought it was him and they went down and caught him and then they took him down there to check the store or something. When they went in to check, they had him handcuffed to the car and some way he run off with the car and run it over into the gravel pit and got loose and got away. He got away from the sheriff's car in that gravel pit and they claim he got a shotgun. They got him and took him up to the hospital up there at Logansport. Now that's when it started.

CASE 218 [27-year-old, white, unmarried male] It was about in '62 or so . . . it must have been in '63 and he was living with some people in Warsaw. I guess he was drinking with them and he tried to steal a car right next door, took it out of the garage. He couldn't get it in reverse or get the emergency brake to stop. . . . The things that I really seen was his actions, just crazy action. I don't know how you'd explain it. Let's put it this way. I know but I don't know how to explain it to you. He mostly threatened people, stuff like that. He never threatened me personally but he did the wife and the kids. I'd come home and it would be all right. I'd tell him to hit the road, I wasn't going to put up with it.

The reactions of network members to the initial unusual behaviors differed in the two networks presented above. In Case 225, three of the four network members viewed the run-in with the law as serious, but it was not necessarily serious from a medical or psychiatric point of view. The patient's father reacted to the attempt to hospitalize his son by obtaining a lawyer and getting the son released from the hospital. In Case 218 the network was unanimous in its judgement that the initial unusual behaviors were not serious.

A third set of descriptions of initial unusual behaviors that lend themselves to nonmedical or nonpsychiatric interpretations involves domestic problems or disputes. A number of Vulnerable Deviant networks described initial problem behaviors that revolved around marital/family disputes:

CASE 240 [56-year-old, white, married female with four children] I don't know if she ever really did lose control of herself. There was a gradual growing on you that she complained that there was something wrong with her and she insisted on being in and out of the hospital and have all kinds of tests made, and she's in fine physical condition, but she still insisted that there was something wrong with her . . . she was married to her present husband when she was sixteen years old. She has been around her husband for such a long time during her life that she does not know of any other kind of life. The whole community in ———— is aware that she is unhappy with her marriage as she is constantly complaining and telling everyone how bad her husband is. She has always been ashamed to be seen with him in public and never wants to go out anywhere with him.

CASE 228 [22-year-old, white, single female] Irene was the kind of person who would listen to people, but if she wasn't in the right mood she would either snap back at people or she would just go in her bedroom and sit. Well, let's go back to the tenth grade. That would be the starting place of where I noticed anything. If she didn't get her way at that time, if things didn't go her way, she picked up and went and ended up in a detention home in South Bend. That same year, in the tenth grade, she had quite a bit of friction with one of her teachers at school. There was friction at home, maybe because of the mixed marriage . . . there was jealousy between the children. [When patient was six years old her mother divorced husband because of pregnancy by another man, the present husband and step-father.] Well, it pertains to her stepfather, mainly. I have been told that the young lady was infatuated with her stepfather and I have been told by many people who have seen them.

The reactions of network members to the initial unusual behaviors in these cases was not uniform. In Case 240, four of the six network members did not see the behaviors as serious. One network member stated: "I don't know; the children had thought it wasn't serious. They thought . . . maybe they got the idea from a doctor . . . that she was putting this on. Well I don't think anybody can put this on, maybe they can, but I don't know. So they just thought that they would just talk her out of it, just bully her out of it some way or other." Another member stated: "No, I didn't think it was serious because I figured that's just the way she was." And another stated: "I thought it was serious, but not from the point of view of her sickness.

It was serious in that it affected other people seriously."

In Case 228, two of the three network members thought the initial unusual behavior serious, but the referent of their concern was the relationship between the patient and her stepfather rather than the psychological problems of the patient.

The final set of cases involving Vulnerable Deviants contains a possibly important pattern of sharp disagreement in the network over whether initial unusual behaviors should be viewed in medical-psychiatric terms or as more understandable, everyday problems. In each of the three cases that follow, some members of each network attempt to "medicalize" the initial unusual behaviors, while others attempt to "normalize" what they have observed:

CASE 236 [41-year-old, white, widowed female with five children] [The initial unusual behavior in this case involves the patient "having an affair with a Mexican" and moving in with him after the death of her husband. She had a fifth child with this man while the four children from the first marriage were in a foster home. Patient apparently neglected children by spending a great deal of time in taverns with her boyfriend.]

One network member: Everything was going fine until this ———— guy came into the picture, and when he started to come in here everything went berserk. Like commanding us to do stuff; he took command of the whole house. Ever since that I lost respect for my Mom, and so did my brothers. And ever since that, we just broke away. So she felt left out and I said that was tough. We had been close but ———— broke it up. That's the darn truth too. If he hadn't come into that picture it would have been one beautiful family. The welfare says that as long as ———— is in the picture she ain't going to get those kids. She says that if she don't get ———— she don't get the kids. It's really just the opposite, if she gives up ———— she gets the kids.

Another member: She didn't strike me as being irrational, but emotionally involved with this person. She did not seem to be unreasonable except with regard to ————. So the only thing unusual I noticed really was the attachment to ————. No, I didn't think it was serious, not at all. I just thought it was an emotional attachment for a woman who is forty-two, who lives alone and wanted to be loved. I don't think she found that love in her family. She found it in ———— even though it was a bogus love.

A second case reveals a similar pattern of sharp disagreement over the meaning attached to the initial unusual behaviors observed:

CASE 415 [46-year-old, white, divorced female with one child]
Person A: I first noticed something last October of 1970. She believed that where she worked the people were trying to discriminate against her

and trying to make her quit her job. But she still worked there. She wouldn't quit her job. She was bound and determined that they wouldn't make her quit her job. She works at a plant and there have been times. . . . There was one specific time when I went over there and talked to the personnel man and he did say that things were rough in there because they were trying to get a union in and I knew they were having a bad time at this time. But like if someone would tell her that she looked ill, she thought that they were trying to make her sick so she'd have to quit work. She also thought that the plant where she worked had hired the FBI to follow her. She also thought that they hired the police to follow her and to check her out.

Person B: She would say things happened out at ——— where she worked that were so hard to believe; yet I believed her, I believed her all the way. I thought she was really telling me the truth and other people don't . . . can't understand this . . . because I've worked in plants and I figured, "I do know things do happen like this." She thought that the doctor gave her a shot of dope and she swore up and down that he gave her a shot of dope. As I get this straight ——— [patient's employer] sent her to a doctor . . . I can't remember his name or anything because she's been to several doctors. I suppose he was a company doctor. He gave her a shot and it swelled all up and there were several different reactions that she had of it. He gave them to her in her leg and she couldn't understand this. She thought that was a weird thing right there. Usually she would have them in the hip or the arm, but he gave it in the leg. It swelled up and got black and blue. Different things like this had happened and she started reading up about dope and stuff in magazines and any article she could get her hands on she'd read about. After reading this stuff she said that she was having the very same symptoms . . . something about her throat and her tongue and so forth and she just swore up and down that the doctor gave her a shot of dope. And she'd tell things about the plant that she said nobody would believe her. They were all picking on her. She said, "I know it sounds stupid, but it's the truth, it really is." Well I've worked out at plants and I know that a lot of times they have favoritism and they might put the oldest one on a rough job if they don't like this person. I've seen it happen myself and so I believed her. I thought, "Well golly, maybe that doctor is crooked." I don't know, there are a lot of quacks around. You never know, you read in the paper all the time where strange things happen. Stranger things than that has happened, that's for sure.

The reaction of both the above networks to the initial unusual behaviors in terms of seriousness and the perceived need for action was divided. Case 236 is a two-person network, and the view of each member indicates the different perspectives on the patient's behavior. The person who thought the patient's emotional entanglements and illegitimate pregnancy were serious tried to get the patient to go to a mental health clinic and tried to get the other network member to assist in achieving this objective. However, assistance was not forthcoming. Instead, the second network member remained firm in his position: "I never really thought she had a mental illness. She seemed for the most part quite reasonable and rational . . . well, not reasonable but rational."

In Case 415, a nine-person network, five members shared the view that the initial unusual behaviors were serious and indicative of mental illness. Although the other four members recognized that many of the things said by the patient were extremely odd, they all held out the possibility that there might be some truth to the charges the patient was making. Consider the following remarks made by network members who were very ambivalent about what the patient was saying: (1) "I could detect a few flaws [in what she said] but generally there were a lot worse people walking around the streets . . . worse than she was"; (2) "It seemed like she got it in her mind that people was against her. Some of these things she said might have been true, but some of them were just kind of unreasonable"; (3) "Well, after a while when this stuff came up and I just couldn't believe it, I thought that there was something wrong somewhere. At first I thought it was serious, but I didn't know if it was true or not."

In our examination of the views of network members associated with Vulnerable Deviants, we have found one dominant pattern in the way network members describe and interpret initial unusual behaviors. Members appear to recognize the existence of problematic behaviors, but they "normalize" those behaviors rather than "medicalize" them. The result is that initial unusual behaviors are accepted as a part of someone's behavioral repertoire and are not viewed as serious from a medical-psychiatric perspective or as requiring some special action outside the network.

Network members' normalization of initial unusual behaviors seems to be the result of five distinct circumstances that concern not only aspects of the behavior but the social context in which the behavior is exhibited.

1. *Initial unusual behaviors are described and interpreted in everyday language* rather than with reference to some more restricted, "private" language reserved for persons already viewed as different or mentally ill. For the most part, people with problems

are viewed as "having let themselves go," having become sloppy in personal grooming, not having taken good care of their kids or their house, or having become difficult to live with.

2. *Some problem behaviors are interpreted as interpersonal disputes*—marital problems, generational conflicts, or problems with co-workers or employers. Such disputes occur in most people's lives, and experiencing them often results in denying that such difficulties are indicative of serious problems in other people's lives.

3. *Some initial unusual behaviors are part of a violation of law.* In such cases, competing contexts determine how the behavior will be interpreted and dealt with. For example, when a network member calls upon a lawyer rather than a doctor or a clinical psychologist for assistance, a particular course of action and a possible outcome are predetermined. While there still exists the possibility that a person caught up in legal machinery will be dealt with in medical-psychiatric terms, the probability of such an outcome is reduced.

4. *In a number of cases problem behaviors occur in connection with status-role transitions*, although such transitions are not used explicitly as a way of explaining or normalizing behavior. Unusual behaviors that follow a divorce or the death of a loved one are often given a conventional character because of the expected grief that accompanies such a transition. In some cases the transitions refer to more pleasant experiences, such as marriage, discharge from military service, or release from prison. Unusual behaviors that follow such transitions are often attributed to lack of preparation for the change or to the need for a period of adjustment.

5. *Avoidance of network conflict* seems to be the main concern of network members in networks where there is sharp disagreement on the meaning of the unusual behavior. In such cases members will generally avoid any action designed to deal with or assist the prepatient.

Protected Patient Patterns. The initial unusual behaviors discussed by members of Protected Patient networks follow a pattern distinctively different from behaviors discussed by members of Vulnerable Deviant networks. The differences are threefold. First, in Protected Patient networks the *content* of the initial unusual behaviors, rather than anything associated with the social context of those behaviors, seems to be the central focus of concern. For example, members do not focus attention on interpersonal disputes associated with unusual behaviors or on any actions that are violations of law. In addition, there is only one instance of the unusual behaviors being associated with any status-role transition.

The second difference concerns the language used to describe the initial unusual behaviors. Protected Patient networks exhibit a greater tendency to use more medical-psychiatric terminology in describing observed behaviors. This difference has implications for the way in which network members respond to the unusual behaviors and affects whether any action is taken.

The third difference is the greater involvement of medical and other professionals in connection with initial unusual behaviors observed in Protected Patient networks. In five of the ten networks the unusual behaviors first observed were followed by an effort to get the pre-patient in to see a doctor.

Let us illustrate our observations about Protected Patient networks by referring to specific case materials. We begin by focusing on the content of the initial unusual behaviors. Five of the ten networks give central attention to the apparent delusions and hallucinations of their pre-patient members:

CASE 412 [54-year-old, white, married male with two children] He asked me if I knew anyone with a green car. Well, we have a green car and he said I think that ———— [patient's wife] has a boyfriend. So then he said that someone was tampering with his car. He said something was wrong with the steering and he had to stop on the highway. He said he was almost run over by a car. He thought someone was trying to kill him. [This patient is a traveling salesman who has been married for thirty-one years and is on the road from Monday through Friday. He has started to accuse his spouse of infidelity and to claim he is not the father of his children.]

CASE 105 [44-year-old, black female, married with two children] Oh, about the first of July I came home and the house is wide open. She was nowhere in sight. Then she said, "We have a cat named Bambi and I killed that cat, I don't trust that cat." Well, we don't have a cat. Then she started to pack my clothes up and packed my daughter's clothes up. She said her mother was dead and I asked how did she know. I asked her if she called and has checked if her mother is sick. She said no. So I said, "Call her." She called, she was having trouble getting her 'cause she changed her number. After that she was walking around the house hollering and screaming at us and at the kids. On top of all this she claimed that everyone was against her, for some kind of reason. She ran out of the house, hollering.

CASE 214 [37-year-old, white, married male with three children] It dates back to his conversion and he heard the Word and took it very literally. He set out to convert everybody in the shop that he worked with.

Some were calm with this and others just wouldn't believe it. He'd preach there on the job and when they didn't receive him well he became suspicious and withdrawn and he hallucinated and at times he was psychotic, he lost touch.

CASE 232 [47-year-old, white male, married with three children]

Person A: The first time I noticed it we were sitting in this living room and he said to me that he was going into private detective work, like an auxiliary police type of thing for the county. I told him to stay out of it, that it wasn't for him and it was dangerous work. He was talking about getting on narcotics squads. He wasn't talking traffic patrol. He was talking narcotic squads and missing persons.

Person B: The way that he would act about certain things, thinking he was capable of doing things that he really wasn't. He would come up with all sorts of wild ideas. Doing electrical work and stuff like that, that I would have thought was silly, but I didn't think he was capable of doing these things. Like he was talking about different big business deals he was making.

CASE 410 [29-year-old, white male, single] This was when he told the story about the hippies being after him. Last spring, he went about a mile and a half through the country in back of his home and wandered up through the woods. These people—they knew his parents very well but didn't recognize him; they hadn't seen him for a while—he looked terrified and told them that some hippies came to his house and beat up his mom and dad, and said he needed help. They called the police and said they would take him home, and they saw that nothing had happened to his parents.

In each of the above cases, network members made an effort, though not in all cases a successful one, to get the pre-patient to a doctor. In three of the cases the effort concerned seeing a psychiatrist rather than simply "a doctor." This reaction is notably different from anything seen in the Vulnerable Deviant networks and is consistent with the medical tone of the language members used to describe the pre-patient's behavior.

Of the remaining five cases of Protected Patients, two involved patients with prolonged, debilitating depression. The behaviors involved withdrawal from friends and family, a great deal of crying, and expressions of guilt, failure, and lack of worth. In both cases the network responded with the judgement that the observed behaviors represented something serious. In one case the pre-patient received assistance at a community mental health center.

Only one case involving Protected Patients resembles the dominant patterns found for Vulnerable Deviants. The case concerned a work-related problem; the pre-patient became depressed and suffered lengthy crying spells because of an inability to cope with interpersonal conflicts with co-workers. However, in contrast to a work-related problem found among Vulnerable Deviants, the network in this case viewed the source of the difficulty as the pre-patient's "mental problems" rather than entertaining the possibility that someone or something external was causing the patient's depression.

Vulnerable Patient and Protected Deviant Patterns. An examination of initial unusual behaviors, and network reaction to those behaviors, for Vulnerable Patients and Protected Deviants will enable us to see if there are any similarities to behaviors and reactions observed for the "pure" types (Vulnerable Deviants and Protected Patients). These comparisons will help us determine whether similarities are due to the extent of social resources patients have or to the kind of symptoms for which patients are hospitalized. For example, if we observe patterns among Vulnerable Patients that are similar to patterns observed for Vulnerable Deviants, we might suspect that the similarity is due to the fact that patients in both categories are low on social resources. If, however, Vulnerable Patients' patterns are similar to those observed for Protected Patients, we might attribute the similarities to common symptoms.

The initial unusual behaviors reported by network members associated with Vulnerable Patients were very varied. They revealed some of the properties of the patterns discussed for each of the "pure" types. About half the patients' observed behaviors were presented in everyday language that stressed interpersonal conflicts, marital disputes, status-role transitions, problems at school, difficulties at work, or excessive drinking. The descriptions closely resembled the initial unusual behaviors reported for Vulnerable Deviants. However, they differed from Vulnerable Deviants in that network members were somewhat more inclined to recommend or seek medical-psychiatric assistance in response to the unusual behavior.

The remaining cases among Vulnerable Patients concerned unusual behaviors that were intrapsychic rather than interpersonal. Depression, hallucinations, and delusions were among the most common behaviors reported. In addition, physical symptoms such as extreme nervousness, fainting, or "spells" were reported. These behaviors are similar to the behaviors that predominated among Protected Patients. The behaviors were described by network members as if they had a high degree of concreteness and directness. They were described without reference to interpersonal relationships that were fused with the behaviors.

Members of Vulnerable Patient networks tended to react to the unusual behaviors by stressing the need for medical-psychiatric attention, regardless of the particular differences in the initial unusual behaviors reported. In this respect, networks of Vulnerable Patients are similar to networks of Protected Patients.

Finding a pattern in initial unusual behaviors of Protected Deviants is difficult because of the small number of cases. Nevertheless, three of the four cases exhibited behaviors based upon interpersonal conflict. One concerned a marital dispute, and the other two involved severe disputes with parents about the pre-patient's friends, language, personal habits, and ideas about politics and work. Reactions by network members to these behaviors were not couched in serious terms, and only one of the networks took action to get the pre-patient to see a doctor. It is noteworthy that in this case the network used medical-psychiatric language to describe the unusual behavior: "She didn't talk insane until last year."

Protected Deviants and their networks show close similarity to Vulnerable Deviants discussed earlier. Since these patient types differ in regard to social resources, similarity in the initial unusual behaviors must be traced to what these two types have in common—namely, the symptoms for which they were ultimately hospitalized.

In sum, an examination of the initial unusual behaviors of Vulnerable Patients and Protected Deviants does not permit an unequivocal statement concerning their similarities to other patient types. Thus, we cannot assert the clear, overriding importance of either a patient's social resources or symptoms in relation to similar or different patterns in initial unusual behaviors.

Total Unusual Behaviors

Throughout most of this chapter the focus has been upon the first instance of unusual pre-patient behavior observed by each network member. In addition, network members were asked to state whether and how frequently they had observed the pre-patient exhibiting any of nineteen behaviors on a preestablished list. They were also asked whether any behaviors on the list had been reported to them by other persons as having been exhibited by the pre-patient. The list of behaviors is as follows:

1. Appeared nervous, tense.
2. Appeared in a daze.
3. Did not make sense when he/she talked.
4. Did not want to talk or be with anyone.
5. Argued with family members.
6. Thought people were talking about him/her.
7. Forgot to do important things.
8. Talked to himself/herself.
9. Said he/she heard voices.
10. Neglected household chores.
11. Did not find work; hung around house all day.
12. Tried to hit or hurt someone.
13. Drank.
14. Damaged and wrecked things.
15. Got into debt; foolish buying.
16. Could not dress or take care of self.
17. Tried to commit suicide.
18. Exposed self indecently.
19. None of above, but seriously bizarre behavior.

The list shifts attention away from the severity or perceived importance of a single behavior to the total amount of unusual behaviors observed by network members directly or reported to them by others. This focus gives a sense of the degree of visibility or obtrusiveness of different pre-patients in their respective networks. It is possible that a network's response to the problem behavior of one of its members is shaped more by the amount of network time consumed by awareness of unusual behaviors than by a single critical incident.

Table 3.4 contains a summary of the average number of unusual behaviors (from the list of nineteen behaviors described above) observed by network members directly and reported to network members by others. In addition, the table shows the average number of behaviors observed "very frequently." The data indicate that Vulnerable Deviants and Protected Deviants have the largest average number of unusual behaviors observed by network members or reported to them by others. In addition, patients from these two types have the largest number of behaviors observed with greatest frequency. The data suggest that the overall visibility of

Table 3.4 Patient Types and Total Unusual Behaviors

Observed Behavior	Vulnerable Patients	Vulnerable Deviants	Protected Patients	Protected Deviants
Mean number of behaviors observed by network members	6.6(92/14)	9.3(177/19)	6.8(68/10)	9.5(38/4)
Mean number of behaviors observed by others	1.7(24/14)	4.6(87/19)	2.3(23/10)	6.5(26/4)
Mean number of behaviors observed "very frequently"	1.0(14/14)	4.4(83/19)	1.9(19/10)	2.8(11/4)

unusual behaviors is more closely related to the kind of symptoms that result in hospitalization (i.e., nonmedical symptoms) than are the social resources of patients. *The data may also suggest that one distinct path to the mental hospital is found among persons who exhibit a large number of problematic behaviors, some of which are expressed in interpersonal disputes and in network conflicts.* In the next chapter we will explore this possibility and others through close examination of circumstances that precipitated hospitalization.

Summary

In this chapter we have examined the recollections of the family, friends, and co-workers of four groups of patients concerning the first behaviors viewed as signs of something amiss. The initial unusual behaviors were not necessarily those for which the patients were ultimately hospitalized. In a few cases the initial unusual behavior was synonymous with the behavior that precipitated hospitalization; however, in almost all cases the initial unusual behaviors were different from, and preceded by a substantial amount of time, the behaviors for which hospitalization ultimately took place. Thus, initial unusual behaviors form a broad background of events and experiences to which network members may refer when observing and interpreting subsequent behavior.

A comparison of the four patient types reveals the sharpest and most consistent differences between Vulnerable Deviants and Protected Patients, and between them and the other types. The differences may be summarized as follows:

1. Social networks of Protected Patients had role structures and socioemotional climates that could serve as potential supports for members. These networks had close ties among members, close ties to the pre-patient, links with nonfamily members, and a recognized leadership and decision-making structure. All other networks had weaker expressions of social-emotional ties and instrumental roles.

2. The initial unusual behaviors reported by members of Vulnerable Deviant networks referred to events and behaviors that had conventional referents and could be normalized with some degree of plausibility. Behaviors involving such things as domestic conflicts, problems with co-workers, and excessive drinking have conventional forms that have probably been experienced by most persons. On the other hand, members of Protected Patient networks reported initial unusual behaviors that emphasized intrapsychic problems (i.e., ideas, thoughts, beliefs) and physical problems (i.e., nerves, spells). Such behaviors occur, in most cases, independently of interpersonal relationships and do not have well-established conventional forms. As a result, medical-psychiatric interpretations are more likely to be used to understand what has been observed.

3. Total unusual behaviors observed by network members or reported to them by others was highest among networks of Vulnerable Deviants and Protected Deviants. The former patient type may best exemplify the dominant propositions of societal reaction theory, which state that persons who have limited resources and who experience many day-to-day problems with living are vulnerable to being *labeled* as having a mental illness.

Endnote

1. W.R. Gove and P. Howell, "Individual Resources and Mental Hospitalization: A Comparison and Evaluation of the Societal Reaction and Psychiatric Perspectives," *American Sociological Review* 39 (February 1974):86–100.

Chapter 4

PATTERN AND PROCESS IN THE COMMITMENT DECISION

In this chapter we examine whether there are discernible patterns in the way in which social networks decide to commit a member to a mental hospital. The patterns observed may be common to all patients and networks, or they may be related to particular characteristics of social networks and patients. In addition to a search for patterns in how social networks decide on commitment, we attempt to uncover specific social processes that appear to shape decisions about hospitalization.

Patterns of Unusual Behavior

In the closing section of Chapter 3, we examined data on the total unusual behaviors of pre-patients as observed by members of the social network or as reported to them by others. These behaviors are more inclusive than specific initial unusual behaviors or critical behaviors that may have precipitated hospitalization. Total unusual behaviors can be taken as an indicator of how visible or obtrusive a pre-patient is within his or her social network. We saw that Vulnerable Deviants and Protected Deviants exhibited the largest number of unusual behaviors (as reported by network members). Thus, visibility of unusual behaviors may be an important feature of one path to the mental hospital.

Our attention now shifts to the substance of the unusual behaviors exhibited by pre-patients, as well as to the relative visibility of the behaviors. We have reduced the nineteen examples of unusual behavior given in Chapter 3 to six general categories as follows:

1. Physical problems:
   appeared nervous, tense
   appeared in a daze
2. Interpersonal problems:
   did not make sense when he/she talked
   did not want to talk or be with anyone
   argued with family members
3. Unusual ideas:
   thought people were talking about him/her
   said he/she heard voices
   talked to himself/herself
4. Role failures:
   forgot to do important things
   neglected household chores
   did not find work
   got into debt
   could not dress or take care of self
5. Aggression:
   tried to hit or hurt someone
   damaged and wrecked things
   tried to commit suicide
6. Norm violations:
   drank to excess
   exposed self indecently

These categories represent behaviors that differ in their apparent severity and in their apparent medical or psychiatric content. Unusual behaviors, or "symptoms," in the first three categories are most prominent in popular views of what constitutes mental illness. Most of the behaviors in the latter three categories seem to represent violations of social standards of proper or expected conduct and do not necessarily have an obvious medical-psychiatric content.

Our first concern is to compare the reported frequency of unusual behaviors across the four patient types. Thus, we can see whether Vulnerable Deviants and Protected Deviants continue to be most visible in all areas of unusual behavior (as reported in Chapter 3), or whether the kind of unusual behavior exhibited differs among patient types.[1] For example, we may predict that Vulnerable Patients and Protected Patients will have the highest reported rates of unusual behavior in the medical-psychiatric symptom categories. Since patients in these two types were ultimately committed for medical symptoms, we might expect that their total unusual behaviors will also be found predominantly in the same areas. We may, by the same logic, predict that Vulnerable Deviants and Protected Deviants, having been committed for nonmedical or nonpsychiatric reasons, will exhibit unusual behaviors concentrated in the nonmedical symptom categories.

Table 4.1 contains a summary of the average (i.e., mean) number of behaviors observed by network members across the four patient types. For example, the category of physical problems contains two specific unusual behaviors ("appeared nervous, tense"; "appeared in a daze"). Network members could have reported observing none, one, or both of these unusual behaviors. Thus, the possible range for the mean scores for networks was zero to two. The mean scores were established in two steps. First, a mean score was established for each network within each patient type by summarizing the number of behaviors reported by each network member. Then a mean score for each patient type was established by summing across the network mean scores and dividing by the number of networks. Thus, a mean score of 1.35 for physical problems associated with Vulnerable Pa-

Table 4.1 Mean Unusual Behaviors Reported by Social Networks

Behaviors	Vulnerable Patients (14)	Vulnerable Deviants (19)	Protected Patients (10)	Protected Deviants (4)
Physical problems (range: 0–2)	1.35	1.54	1.33	1.56
Interpersonal problems (range: 0–3)	1.47	1.72	1.27	1.97
Unusual ideas (range 0–3)	1.19	1.15	1.03	1.20
Role failure (range: 0–5)	1.08	2.46	1.03	2.48
Aggression (range: 0–3)	0.59	0.85	0.62	0.34
Norm violations (range: 0–2)	0.12	0.40	0.42	0.23

tients indicates that in the fourteen networks associated with Vulnerable Patients, each network member on the average reported observing 1.35 (out of a possible two) unusual behaviors.

Several general patterns can be observed in the table. First, the rates of reported unusual behavior for all four patient types are almost always highest in the medical categories ("Physical problems," "Interpersonal problems," "Unusual ideas"). The nonmedical category "Role failure" has rates that exceed those reported in the medical categories in two instances. Rates in the categories of "Aggression" and "Norm violations" are substantially lower than those reported in all other areas. A second general pattern observed in the table is that the rates of reported unusual behavior are generally lower for Vulnerable Patients and Protected Patients than for Vulnerable Deviants and Protected Deviants. This pattern is most pronounced in the categories of "Role failure" and "Interpersonal problems." Differences found in other areas are smaller or inconsistent.

The table shows little evidence to support the expectation that the highest reported rates of total unusual behavior will be in areas consistent with the symptoms for which patients were eventually hospitalized. Vulnerable Patients and Protected Patients, who were hospitalized for medical symptoms, do not have higher rates of medically oriented unusual behaviors than do Vulnerable Deviants and Protected Deviants, who were hospitalized for nonmedical symptoms. There is some support for the converse prediction, however; Vulnerable Deviants and Protected Deviants, hospitalized for a variety of nonmedical symptoms, do show a tendency toward higher rates of unusual behaviors in the nonmedical areas. This tendency is especially pronounced with respect to "Role failure" and to some extent (for Vulnerable Deviants only) with respect to "Aggression" and "Norm violations."

The broadest supportable generalization from these data continues to be that patient types, with respect to total unusual behaviors reported by network members, differ in the extent of visibility of unusual behaviors across all categories. The data are consistent with a view that some people are committed to hospitals because they exhibit a large number and variety of unusual behaviors (e.g., Vulnerable Deviants) rather than a small number of serious behaviors. The frequency of problematic behavior, rather than the nature of the behavior itself, helps shape decisions to hospitalize patients.

It is possible that the frequency with which all unusual behavior is exhibited is not as important as the particular patterns of behavior exhibited by pre-patients. Certain combinations of unusual behaviors (rather than total behavior or a single overriding behavior) may make a pre-patient most visible or most problematic to network members. For example, both physical problems and role failure may be exhibited by all patients or by a particular type of patient. If so, we might see the pre-patient's basic problem as physical in origin (tension, nervousness) but as expressing itself as a network problem in the form of inability to carry out role responsibilities (work, household duties).

There is only one distinct pattern in the data on pairs of frequently occurring unusual behavior (see Appendix A, Table A.1). Vulnerable Deviants are the only patients who exhibit a relatively high number of pairs of unusual behaviors from across the six categories of unusual behavior. The paired behaviors, in the order of most frequently occurring pairs, are as follows:

Interpersonal problems—Aggression.
Interpersonal problems—Role failure.
Interpersonal problems—Unusual ideas.
Interpersonal problems—Physical problems.

Given the constituent items of the category of interpersonal problems, the link between interpersonal problems, on the one hand, and aggression and unusual ideas, on the other, is to be expected. This category contains items such as "didn't make sense when he/she talked" and "argued with family members." These items do not automatically imply "aggression" or "unusual ideas," but the connection is highly probable. The link between interpersonal problems and role failure or physical problems is less likely to be traced to similarity in the items used for measuring these unusual behaviors. Interpersonal problems are likely to have their origin in role failures and in physical problems.

Another matter to consider in a discussion of total unusual behaviors is whether the behaviors, in addition to being visible, are perceived by network members as having created problems for persons associated with the patient. All network members were asked if any of the patient's unusual behaviors had created problems for anyone in the family or the community—relatives, neighbors, employers, co-workers, police, or others. The number of groups mentioned by network members can be taken as a measure of the extent to which a pre-patient's unusual behaviors were perceived to create problems.

Of all the groups for whom the pre-patient's unusual behaviors may have caused problems, the family was most frequently mentioned (67 percent of network members), followed by police (44 percent of network members). A much smaller percentage of network members (18 percent) indicated that problems had been created for employers. Fifteen percent cited problems for neighbors, and 7 percent for co-workers. The average number of groups mentioned by network members from each patient type was as follows:

Vulnerable Patients — 1.2 groups
Vulnerable Deviants — 1.6 groups
Protected Patients   — 1.4 groups
Protected Deviants   — 1.8 groups

Although the differences were small, the unusual behavior of Deviants created problems for more groups than did behavior reported for any of the other patient types. Vulnerable Deviants and Protected Deviants were thus more visible with respect to the frequency of unusual behaviors, and their behaviors created more problems for other persons and groups.

Involvement of the police with the unusual behavior of pre-patients exhibited some noteworthy patterns across the patient types. Networks were classified according to whether one half or more of their members indicated that the pre-patient's unusual behavior had created problems for the police. Fifty percent of Vulnerable Patient networks (seven of fourteen) and 40 percent of Protected Patient networks (four of ten) reported that their pre-patient's behavior had involved the police. In contrast, about 70 percent of Vulnerable Deviant networks (thirteen of nineteen) and 75 percent of Protected Deviant networks (three of four) had pre-patients whose behaviors had involved the police.

The result of our search for patterns in the unusual behaviors exhibited by pre-patients thus provided the following findings: Patients hospitalized for what appeared to be nonmedical reasons (Vulnerable Deviants and Protected Deviants) were reported by network members to have exhibited more unusual behaviors than patients committed for medical reasons (Vulnerable Patients and Protected Patients). The greater visibility of the Deviants' unusual behavior was also expressed in identifiable combinations and created more problems for other persons (especially police) with whom the pre-patient came in contact. For Deviants, the path to the mental hospital seems characterized by greater visibility of unusual behaviors and greater negative effects of such behaviors on other persons.

Symptom Selection by Networks

In Chapters 2 and 3 we saw that persons committed for mental illness exhibited a wide range of behaviors considered problematic by persons with whom they were closely associated. Within the social networks in which pre-patients resided, considerable variation existed in the particular problematic behaviors observed by members. Earlier in this chapter we described the broad range of different types of behaviors exhibited by pre-patients and observed by network members.

Despite the great variety of unusual behaviors reported as exhibited by pre-patients over a period of time prior to hospitalization, many networks eventually focus their collective attention on a much narrower set of behaviors that serve as the basis for thinking about hospitalization. This narrowing focus of concern was evident when we examined the official reasons for commitment reported in hospital documents or in commitment papers. For all four patient types, a limited set of problematic behaviors was specified by network members as the basis for hospitalization.

These two facts—the variety of unusual behaviors exhibited by pre-patients and the emphasis on selected behaviors in relation to the hospitalization decision—raise the question of how and why social networks select the particular unusual behaviors that become the focus of concern. The possible reasons are numerous. In the following sections we consider a number of characteristics associated with the four patient types that may help us understand the different emphases networks place on the most problematic unusual behaviors. These characteristics are (1) educational and occupational status of the networks, (2) quality of the network's knowledge of mental illness, (3) the network's tendency to maintain "social distance" from mental patients, and (4) degree of the network's tolerance for deviance.

Socioeconomic Status

One factor that can influence a network's choice of unusual behaviors as the focus of their concern is the socioeconomic standing of network members. Persons who are better educated or employed in higher-status occupations will probably have greater exposure to information about mental illness and its various symptoms. They should therefore select focal symptoms that have medical-psychiatric content of the sort found among Vulnerable Patients and Protected Patients. Network members for these two patient types should be of higher socioeconomic status, while members associated with Vulnerable Deviants and Protected Deviants should have lower socioeconomic status.

Network members were classified by occupation according to whether they were "upper white-collar" (e.g., teacher, manager); "lower white-collar" (e.g., salesperson, secretary); "upper blue-collar" (e.g., electrician, carpenter); or "lower blue-collar" (e.g., farm laborer, machine operator). Networks that had half or more of their members in upper or lower white-collar occupations were considered to have high social standing. Six of ten Protected Patient networks (60 percent) and three of fourteen Vulnerable Patient networks (21 percent) were predominantly white-collar, while five of nineteen Vulnerable Deviant networks (26 percent) and one of four Protected Deviant networks (25 percent) were of comparable standing.

An additional aspect of occupational standing that we considered was simply being in the labor force, regardless of the status of the person's occupation. Vulnerable Patient and Protected Patient networks had the fewest number of adult members who were unemployed or not in the labor force (1.1 persons), while Vulnerable Deviant and Protected Deviant networks had 1.6 and 2.0 persons, respectively, not in the labor force.

We used a combination of two measures to establish the educational status of social networks. Networks in which half or more of the members had at least high school diplomas *and* at least one member with "some college" were classified as having high educational status. Six of fourteen Vulnerable Patient networks (43 percent) and seven of ten Protected Patient networks (70 percent) fit the criteria for high educational status, while Vulnerable Deviants and Protected Deviants had nine of nineteen networks (47 percent) and two of four networks (50 percent), respectively, of high educational status.

In general, the occupational and educational status of networks associated with Protected Patients was notably higher than in other networks. However, the fact that Vulnerable Patient networks were not different in socioeconomic composition from Vulnerable Deviant and Protected Deviant networks suggests that a network's selection of the unusual behaviors of greatest concern is not solely related to a network's occupational and educational characteristics.

Knowledge of Mental Illness

A second factor that may influence a network's choice of symptoms is the quality of members' knowledge of mental illness. This factor was measured through use of the Nunnally scale, which consists of ten statements considered true or false according to expert knowledge.[2] The statements are as follows:

- There is not much that can be done for a person who develops a mental disorder.

  Most people in mental hospitals speak in words that can be understood.
- Mental health is largely a matter of trying to control your emotions.
- If a person concentrates on happy memories, he will not be bothered by unpleasant things in the present.
- Almost any disease that attacks the nervous system is likely to bring on insanity.

  X-rays of the head will not tell whether a person is likely to become insane.
- Psychiatrists try to teach mental patients to hold in their strong emotions.
- The main job of the psychiatrist is to recommend hobbies and other ways for the patient to occupy his mind.
- The insane laugh more than normals.

  A change of climate seldom helps an emotional disorder.

Respondents' agreement with items marked by a bullet was judged to reflect a low degree of knowledge of mental illness, while agreement with unmarked items was judged to reflect a high degree of knowledge. Network members responded to the items on a five-point scale ranging from "strongly agree" to "strongly disagree."

A network's knowledge of mental illness was determined by combining members' responses to the ten items listed above. When half or more of a network's members had scores that reflected a high degree of knowledge of mental illness, the network was classified as exhibiting a high degree of knowledge.

Since Vulnerable Patients and Protected Patients had been admitted for medical-psychiatric symptoms, we can expect that the social networks of these patients would exhibit a high degree of knowledge of mental illness. Six of fourteen Vulnerable Patient networks (43 percent) exhibited a high degree of knowledge, while all but one of the Protected Patient networks (90 percent) had a high degree of knowledge.

In the case of Vulnerable Deviant and Protected Deviant patients committed for a variety of types of deviance (i.e., behavior lacking clear medical-psychiatric content), we can expect to find social networks that exhibit a lesser degree of knowledge of mental illness. Network members who lack such knowledge are less likely to "medicalize" the problematic and unusual behaviors they observe. Eight of nineteenVulnerable Deviant networks (42 percent) exhibited a high degree of knowledge of mental illness, as did two of four Protected Deviant networks (50 percent).

Once again Protected Patient networks differed sharply from the others in exhibiting the highest degree of knowledge of mental illness. There was no indication that networks with patients committed for nonmedical symptoms (Deviants) had less knowledge than did Vulnerable Patient networks whose patients exhibited medical symptoms. In short, the distinctiveness of Protected Patient networks has been demonstrated, while no overall clear relationship was evident between a network's knowledge of mental illness and its tendency to select medical- or deviant-type symptoms as the basis for hospitalization.

Attitudes toward Mental Patients

Social networks may differ in terms of their beliefs, stereotypes, and fears about persons with mental illness. One form of negative orientation toward the mentally ill is expressed in the desire to maintain "social distance" from them by excluding them from a variety of conventional social relationships. Network members were asked to respond to seven items that measure a tendency to maintain social distance from *former* mental patients. The specific items are as follows:

- It would be wise to discourage former patients of a mental hospital from entering your neighborhood.
- It would be unwise to encourage the close friendship of someone who had been in a mental hospital.

I would be willing to sponsor a former patient of a mental hospital for membership in my favorite club or society.

If I were a personnel manager, I would be willing to hire a former patient of a mental hospital.

- If I were responsible for renting apartments in my building, I would hesitate to rent living quarters to someone who had been in a mental hospital.
- You should strongly discourage your children from marrying someone who was formerly in a mental hospital.
- It would be unwise to trust a former mental patient with your children.

Respondents were asked to select answers from a five-point scale ranging from "strongly agree" to "strongly disagree." Agreement with items marked by a bullet indicated a tendency to maintain social distance from former mental patients. Agreement with unmarked items indicated a tendency not to maintain social distance from former patients.

When half or more of a network's members had scores that reflected a tendency to maintain greater social distance from former patients, the network was classified as having attitudes of high social distance. The other networks were judged to exhibit attitudes of low social distance.

Networks associated with Vulnerable Patients and Protected Patients revealed attitudes reflective of low social distance. Moreover, among Protected Patients all ten networks had attitudes of low social distance. Vulnerable Deviants had eight of nineteen networks (42 percent) with attitudes of low social distance, and Protected Deviants had two of four networks (50 percent) with such attitudes.

Once again, networks of Protected Patients appeared sharply different from the others. Networks of the three remaining patient types were very similar insofar as the number whose attitudes reflected a desire to maximize social distance with former patients approximately equaled the number who reflected a desire to minimize such relationships.

Tolerance for Deviance

The final factor that can influence a network's reaction to symptoms is the degree of tolerance for persons who exhibit behavior that may cause problems for themselves and others. Our approach to measuring a network's tolerance for deviance involved the use of six hypothetical cases describing persons with different degrees of psychological problems.[3] Each case was judged clinically to represent, respectively, (1) paranoia, (2) simple schizophrenia, (3) anxiety neurosis, (4) alcoholism, (5) compulsive phobia, and (6) juvenile character disorder (see Appendix B for the specific case descriptions). Respondents were asked to react to each case in terms of the following responses: (1) There may be something wrong with him, but it's not mental illness and not serious; (2) He has mental illness, but it's not serious; (3) He hasn't got mental illness, but it is serious; and (4) He has a serious mental illness. Network members were also asked to describe the course of action that should be taken in each case. Answers were given in terms of the following responses: (1) He should be admitted to a mental hospital; (2) He should probably get help outside the hospital from a doctor who specializes in mental illness; (3) He should get help from his family and friends; (4) He just needs a rest, like a vacation; and (5) He doesn't need any help; he can get over it himself.

Table 4.2 contains a summary of the reactions of network members from the four patient types to the six hypothetical cases of psychological problems. Network members associated with Pro-

Table 4.2   Tolerance for Deviance: Social Network Reactions to Six Hypothetical Cases of Psychological Disorder

	Vulnerable Patients (14)	*Vulnerable Deviants* (19)	*Protected Patients* (10)	*Protected Deviants* (4)
Mean number of cases judged to have "serious mental illness"	2.2	2.6	1.8	2.2
Mean number of cases judged to have "serious mental illness" or "mental illness but not serious"	3.4	3.7	2.8	4.2
Mean number of cases recommended for admission to mental hospital	1.8	2.1	1.6	1.8
Mean number of cases recommended for mental hospital or to psychiatrist outside hospital	4.3	4.6	3.5	4.4
Number of network members	(53)	(84)	(46)	(16)

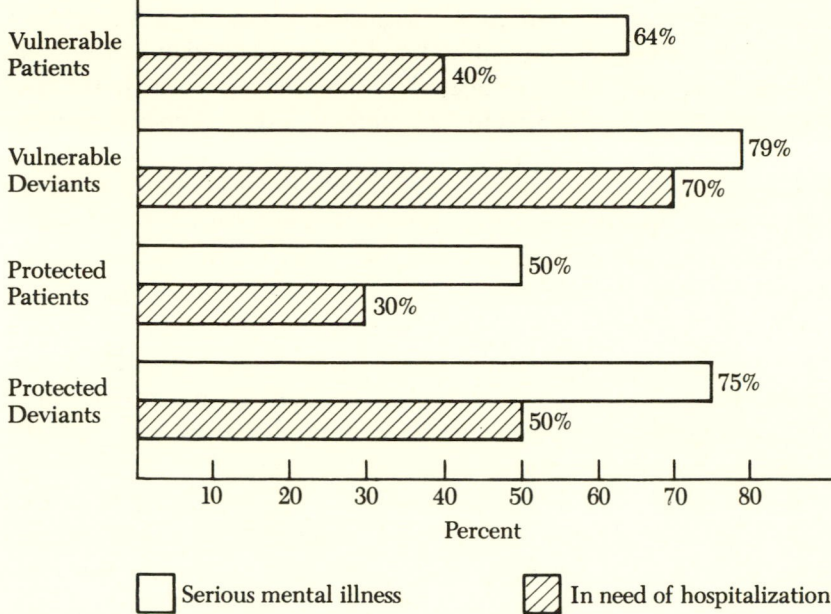

Figure 4.1   Percentage of Social Networks Judging Paranoid and Schizophrenic Cases as "Serious Mental Illness" and "In Need of Hospitalization."

tected Patients judged the fewest cases as "serious mental illness," while Vulnerable Deviant networks judged the most cases as "serious mental illness." Network members associated with Protected Patients also judged the fewest cases as "serious mental illness" or "mental illness but not serious."

Another way of estimating the tolerance for deviance in different social networks is to look at reactions of network members to the most serious of the six cases listed above. Clinical judgements on the cases identified the paranoid and simple schizophrenic cases most serious.

Figure 4.1 summarizes the reaction of networks to the two most serious cases. Half of the Protected Patient networks identified the paranoid and schizophrenic cases as serious mental illness. In contrast, about four fifths of Vulnerable Deviant networks (fifteen of nineteen), two thirds of Vulnerable Patient networks (nine of fourteen), and three fourths of Protected Deviant networks (three of four) identified the clinically serious cases as serious mental illness.

Clearly, the Protected Patient networks appeared to have the greatest tolerance for deviance, at least as reflected in reactions to the hypothetical cases of psychological disorder. The Vulnerable Deviant networks, on the other hand, seemed to exhibit the least tolerance for deviance, as indicated by the relatively large number of cases they judged as serious mental illness, and by their reactions to the two clinically serious cases.

Table 4.2 also reports the average number of cases network members recommended for admission to a mental hospital. Once again, network members associated with Protected Patients recommended the fewest cases for hospitalization, and networks of Vulnerable Deviants recommended the greatest number, although the differences were small. When the recommended action was expanded to include seeing a psychiatrist outside a hospital, the mean number of cases recommended for such action increased sharply, although the pattern across patient types remained the same.

Recommendations for hospitalization in the two clinically serious cases indicated that only three of ten Protected Patient networks had a majority of members suggesting hospitalization for the two most serious cases, compared to seven of ten Vulnerable Deviant networks, four of ten Vulnerable Patient networks, and five of ten Protected Deviant networks. Tolerance for deviance, as reflected in a lesser desire to seek hospitalization in clinically serious cases, was thus greatest among Protected Patient networks and lowest among Vulnerable Deviant networks. (See Figure 4.1.)

Patterns of Symptom Selection

In the preceding sections we have attempted to determine whether selected characteristics of social networks could be responsible for the way in which networks select the particular symptoms of concern to them. The characteristics for comparison across networks included socioeconomic standing, knowledge of mental illness, attitudes toward mental patients, and tolerance for deviance.

Networks associated with Protected Patients were markedly different from the others; they had higher socioeconomic standing, greater knowledge of mental illness, greater tolerance for deviance, and more favorable attitudes toward the mentally ill. Vulnerable Patient networks were most similar to those of Protected Patients, especially with regard to greater tolerance for deviance. The committing symptoms for patients from both of these types were medical or psychiatric in content. The choice of such symptoms as the focus of concern was consistent with the networks' higher socioeconomic standing and greater knowledge of mental illness. Such networks would be more likely to think about unusual behaviors in medical terms rather than to view them simply as "tolerable problems." In addition, any impaired role behavior of persons with high social position (e.g., inability to work) might pose a more serious problem to the network and thereby encourage quick action to deal with the problem.

Contingencies and Critical Incidents that Shape Commitment

We now know that pre-patients have exhibited a wide range of unusual behaviors that have sometimes extended over a period of years. The long-standing character of these problem behaviors raises the question of why the decision to hospitalize is finally made at a particular time, after long periods of network tolerance of unusual behavior. In Chapter 3 we found that the commitment decision follows initial unusual behaviors rather quickly for patients with medical symptoms as the basis for commitment. Relatively quick commitment happens especially with Protected Patients (i.e., patients with medical symptoms and high resources). Vulnerable Deviants and Protected Deviants, on the other hand, remain in their families and communities while exhibiting a greater number and variety of unusual behaviors.

In this section we examine the circumstances surrounding the commitment decision in search of social situations or critical incidents that reduce a social network's ability to sustain a problematic member. Reduced capacity of a network to support one of its members may be due to changes within the network that subject its members to new problems or to new pressures on the network from external sources that require a new solution to an old problem. First we examine the situation of the multiproblem network faced with increasing problems and limited resources for dealing with them. Next we look at the impact of incidents like death and divorce, which alter the structure of networks. Finally we attempt to identify the circumstances in which outside professionals attempt to intervene and "force" social networks to act when they might otherwise not do so.

Multiproblem Networks

A multiproblem network is one in which persons other than the pre-patient are themselves experiencing problems with living. Such networks come under pressure from several sources within the network and from elements outside the network. One type of multiproblem network contains a problematic member who has been sustained for some time within the network and for whom certain adaptations have already occurred. The appearance of new problems connected with the pre-patient, to which the network has not adapted, puts more strain on the network than it is prepared to handle. A variant of this type is a network in which a member other than the long-standing problem member (the pre-patient) begins to have problems. This situation also puts pressure on the network and requires a new adaptation.

Seven of the forty-seven networks we examined contained clear indications of being multiproblem networks. Interestingly, these seven cases were found among Vulnerable Patients and Vulnerable Deviants, both of which are types with limited social resources. The multiproblem cases involved networks where persons other than the pre-patient were (1) former mental patients, (2) involved in excessive drinking, (3) sexually exploiting the pre-patient, or (4) involved in strained relationships (e.g., marital disputes) with other network members. In at least two of these cases, commitment was the network's way of recognizing and handling their growing problems. In the other five cases we must infer a link between multiple problems and commitment. Statements linking hospitalization to network problems are illustrated in the following remarks from network members:

CASE 228   I think it has to be total removal [commitment], because their house was just chaos.

CASE 101   All her problems are at home. It became impossible to be under the same roof.

CASE 421   There is a lot of conflict in the family. Parents are involved in a destructive relationship.

CASE 401   Practically all the family drinks, and there is an indication that schizophrenic behavior may run in the context of the family. Violence abounds . . .

In all but one of the seven multiproblem networks, the pre-patient was living with his or her parents (both parents in three cases, and mother in the other three cases). The networks were smaller on the average (4.6 members) than were other networks for any of the patient types (see Table 3.2). Moreover, the number of persons with whom the pre-patient lived was very small—one or more parents and occasionally a sibling. Small families probably have greater difficulty sustaining more than one problem member.

Shrinking Networks

Change in the composition and size of networks seems to influence the commitment decision. Divorce or death of a central figure in a network can change a network's capacity to sustain members with problems. In some cases networks shrink when older children move out on their own, often to avoid the stress of living with problem parents or siblings. When a network shrinks, greater stress is put on the remaining family members because of lost economic and psychological resources.

Four cases contained evidence of a commitment decision resulting from an unanticipated change in the network—a change that reduced support for the pre-patient. Three of the four patients in these cases were types with limited resources (Vulnerable Patients and Vulnerable Deviants). A clear example of commitment related to the death of a key member of the network is found in the following case:

CASE 414 *Sister:* After Mother's death she [the pre-patient] went back to live in her home [where she had lived with her mother] by herself. She had a little money, and she was going to try to get work and get some money because she wanted to stay in her own home. She didn't want to stay with me. She moved in and out of here eight times. We moved her furniture and bed and things and tried to get her settled, because Mother's death was a great shock to her. It was a great shock to all of us but especially to her because she lived with her and was dependent on her.

Brother: She had a run-away pattern. Mom was the only one who had any control over her. We would beg her on our knees to get into the car and come back after she had run away, and we'd go get Mother, and Mother would tell her to get in here and she'd get in there and it would be all over. Mother has always had the control over her, so we didn't have much trouble with her until after Mother died. Mother had the supreme control. She was the supreme commander. We didn't cross Mother.

Sister: Years ago I wanted her to see a psychiatrist. Between Rose [the pre-patient] and I, we decided that she needed some kind of help. So I talked it over with my mother and she said that I was the one that was crazy, not Rose. So I never brought it up again and Rose didn't either, and that was it.

Following is another case that reveals a link between a death in the network and the commitment decision:

CASE 209 *Sister:* The one that made all the decisions was her [the pre-patient's] father. He was the leader in that family. When he died four years ago, that's when all this trouble started. After her father passed away I took her to Dr. B———, a psychiatrist. I told him about her problems, but he didn't give or do a thing for her. . . . Although I would have had her home here, I wouldn't want to leave her alone for a minute. I work five hours a day as a waitress; it's so hard to get anyone to stay with her. It made me so sick. I should have been in the hospital myself. She stopped cooking. I'd come home from work, I'd say, "Marie, what will we have for supper?" She'd say, "Let's have some breakfast food." She wouldn't work in the house. She wouldn't go to the mailbox. I just couldn't understand this. I didn't know what to do, where to go, who to consult. No one knew how miserable I was.

The next case concerns a divorce in a small, three-person network made up of husband, wife, and ten-year-old child. The divorce left the pre-patient (the husband) living alone as a total isolate. Problems that existed before the divorce became magnified and more visible to others outside the closed family setting:

CASE 412 *Wife:* John has always done unusual things. People accepted his bizarre behavior, until recently. Because of John's behavior, I filed for divorce. That's when he moved out of the house into the Carmel Motel. When he was there his behavior was bizarre. I understand from the owners that one day he couldn't go in his bathroom and shave. He came down to the manager's in his shorts and wanted to shave there in his room. He also went next door to Reverend Wilson at 12:30 A.M., 3:30 A.M., and then again at 5:30 A.M., and he wanted the reverend to come back into the house with him. . . . Reverend Wilson said John had lost touch with reality. . . . [He] thought John should be committed.

The final case of a shrinking network cannot be documented with specific statements. The pre-patient was a young adult living with mother and four adult siblings. Over the course of about two years, each of the siblings moved out of the house to get places of their own. It cannot be demonstrated that the problems of the pre-patient were responsible for the siblings' decisions to leave the family, although that was the implication of their actions. After everyone had left, the mother and the pre-patient were left on their own, without whatever social, emotional, and economic support had formerly been provided by other family members. Presumably, the mother's decision to seek hospitalization for the pre-patient was influenced by the changing composition of the family.

Networks that Involve Outside Professionals

In five of the networks studied, the decision regarding hospitalization appeared to have been instigated or shaped by professionals outside the social network.[4] Three of the cases involved Protected Patients, and two involved Vulnerable Deviants. Thus, the role of "outsiders" in shaping the commitment decision does not appear to have been related to the kind of symptoms that produced commitment or to the social resources of the patient.

In three of the cases the outsiders involved were police. The pre-patient in each case became involved in a situation that came to the attention of the police. While the families of the pre-patients were apparently prepared to treat the situation as just another problem, the police either directly involved the mental health system or strongly urged the family to seek professional assistance. The following case summaries illustrate the involvement of outsiders with the social network:

CASE 106   The pre-patient is well known to the police for frequent automobile accidents and for having served time in prison for auto theft. The critical incident or situational problem involves neighbors of the pre-patient, who call the police about a prowler in the neighborhood. The police arrive and find the pre-patient walking in the alley between houses. No charges are made, as the pre-patient cannot be identified as the prowler. The police talk to the pre-patient's mother, who reports that they warned her that she had better learn to "handle him" and "take him to a mental doctor." The police also alert the pre-patient's parole officer, who tells the family that in order to avoid returning to prison, the pre-patient must have psychiatric help. The pre-patient's mother states: "We had to promise to take him for treatment once a month." The pre-patient becomes an out-patient at a community mental health center. Within six months he is committed to a state mental hospital.

CASE 214   The pre-patient's problems have been noticed for about three and a half years. The family had come to accept his withdrawn behavior and his obsession with religion, which involved efforts to convert friends and co-workers. None of these problems prompted network members to consider medical-psychiatric assistance. The pre-patient is arrested for drunken driving and is charged with assault and battery and resisting arrest by the police. He is sentenced to thirty days in jail, during which time he is committed to the state mental hospital. Network members are extremely vague about what happened in prison. One network member states that he was having a hard time of it in jail and probably recognized "that he was in pretty bad shape, but I imagine he was forced to go to the hospital from the jail after the doctor had seen him."

CASE 219   The pre-patient is a 38-year-old male, living at home with his parents on their small farm. He has been difficult to live with for many years, so his parents report. The difficulties have mainly involved constant arguments about the farm and the pre-patients's failure to meet parental expectations. The parents believe their son is mentally retarded and recently has become more threatening to them. In one argument the pre-patient attempts to hit his father with a chair and strikes his mother. The parents call the sheriff, who puts the father in touch with a local judge for advice. The judge recommends a physician, who suggests hospitalization. (The father states: "The doctor insisted.")

In each of the above cases, the involvement of "outsiders"—that is, of police and physicians—was clearly related to the decision to hospitalize the network member with problems. It is not simply that the outsiders helped to identify the problem, for each network was well aware that one of its members had a problem. Rather, the outsiders seemed to make it possible for the network to consider commitment to a mental hospital as a way of dealing with the problem. While network members undoubtedly had considered hospitalization in the past, they were now able to transfer some of the responsibility for a decision too difficult for those closest to the pre-patient.

In the remaining two cases involving "outsiders," the decision by network members was precipitated by an incident involving, but not initiated by, the pre-patient. Had the incident not occurred, the pre-patient would still have had his or her "problem" but might not have been hospitalized for it. The cases are described as follows:

CASE 236   Pre-patient is a 41-year-old woman with five children. Three years after the death of her husband, the pre-patient (according to her grown son) "starts having an affair with a Mexican," who fathers her fifth child. The pre-patient's "loose" behavior and alleged neglect of her younger children results in placement of her children in foster homes.

Social worker: Her affair with ———— resulted in her fifth child, although he has refused to help support it. She has continued her relationship with

him, although her children express great opposition to him. Mrs. ———
and her children are living under a great deal of physical and psychological
stress. To begin with, their housing situation is extremely poor. The home
they live in is a three-room structure consisting of a living room, a kitchen,
and one bedroom. It is very dilapidated and in need of much repair. The
wooden floors are bare and black with age. The plasterboard walls have
numerous holes and chips in them. To my knowledge, the ———s have
lived here for eighteen years or over.

*The pre-patient's oldest son relates an incident in which he alleges that
his mother and her boyfriend are down in an area of the city where there
are houses of prostitution:* I went down there with a squad car of police and
we got the guy to get my ma out of there in time before that raid started.
When I got hold of her she was hysterical, she was pushing me around.
Because she was pushing me around I was even slapping her down. . . .
She'd get more violent and started giving me some of my own medicine
back. So I called that lawyer and he said the best thing I could do would be
to come out and sign the commitment papers.

CASE 218   Pre-patient's problem behaviors appear to have started in his
late teens. His parents divorced when he was nine, and he lived with his
mother until age fifteen, when he moved in with his father. This move was
apparently precipitated by a run-in with the law involving an auto theft.
The pre-patient spent a year at a state farm for boys. After his father's death
(when pre-patient was nineteen) the pre-patient took to traveling around
the country hitchhiking and having frequent problems with the law. He
was arrested in Washington, D.C. and spent some time in jail in Oklahoma.
(Network members are extremely vague about the incidents: "He was
picked up on government property in D.C." "[In Oklahoma City] they said
it was for outraging public decency.") After living in California for a time,
the pre-patient returned to the Midwest. While hitchhiking in Chicago he
was beaten up and stabbed.

Mother: I hadn't seen him for some time and I got a phone call at 2:30
A.M. They said that he had been stabbed seriously and asked me if I could
come. I said no, that my husband was out of work and that there was no way
that I could come. Two weeks and two days later I got a phone call from
——— [son] that welfare had put him on a bus and sent him here. I
absolutely refused to try to take care of him, especially after he told me
some of the things he did. He got out of bed, he had a temporary cast on,
and he tried to walk and he collapsed and they had to pick him up and put
him back in bed. I knew then that he was still mentally ill because anyone
with any sense should know better than that. He had a collapsed lung, a
ligament in his right knee cut, and he had twelve serious stab wounds.
That's what they said but he had more than that. I counted thirty-five holes
in his clothes. I could see he was not well. You could just look at him. He
told me about this. When he came home he had a walking cast on. I could

not take care of him because I had double club feet when I was born and I had a lot of arthritis this winter and I wasn't hardly able to get around and do the things that had to be done here. That's when I went up here to the mental health clinic and they called the hospital and had him admitted.

We have thus identified sixteen networks in which the decision to commit a member can be traced to processes shaped by network characteristics. Multiproblem networks, shrinking networks, and situations within the network that attract the attention of professionals all seem to lead network members to decide upon commitment. Networks with these characteristics have greater difficulty in sustaining a member with problems or in resisting pressure from legal or medical authorities. In Chapter 6 we shall see whether patients from these types of social networks are likely to be released from hospitalization.

Pre-Patient's View of the Hospitalization Decision

While social networks are influenced by some forces to choose hospitalization and by other forces to disregard hospitalization as a solution, the role of the pre-patient and his or her reaction to the idea of hospitalization can be a central feature of the commitment decision. A pre-patient who is strongly opposed to the idea of entering a mental hospital may deter a network from considering the matter, especially if the pre-patient has some power in the network (e.g., sole provider or head of household). On the other hand, pre-patients who appear to accept network judgements about their illness and the need for hospitalization may encourage networks to move toward commitment much more easily.

Another process that contributes to the commitment decision is what was referred to in Figure 1.1 as stabilization of the deviant role—that is, a gradual acceptance by the pre-patient of the network's concerns about and definitions of the pre-patient's illness. This acceptance is reflected in what Erving Goffman refers to as a "loss of the props of normality"[5]—all the activities (shopping, cooking, playing with one's children, performing household chores) that comprise elements of "normal" social roles. The loss of such "props" may be directly related to the pre-patient's problems, but it may also be a way of expressing acceptance of illness. Accepting the "sick role" usually includes a reduction of responsibilities and activities.

Our first concern in this section is to look for differences across patient types in the extent to which pre-patients lose their "props of normality" prior to hospitalization and to examine differences in pre-patient reactions to network allegations of illness and the need for hospitalization. This investigation will permit us to see if the severity of the committing symptoms or the vulnerability (i.e., social resources) of the pre-patient is related to the process of "stabilizing the deviant role." Our second concern is to see if a connection exists between the characteristics of social networks and pre-patients' reactions to network definitions. Close, supportive networks may have greater ability to get their pre-patients to accept their illness and the need for hospitalization. Such ability could be due to the greater trust and support that exists between the pre-patient and the network members, as well as to a belief that the interests of the pre-patient are of primary concern to the network. On the other hand, in nonsupportive, "weak" networks pre-patients may suspect the motives of friends or kin who are trying to hospitalize them.

All network members were asked to indicate whether or not the pre-patient agreed that he or she had a mental illness. They were also asked if the pre-patient agreed with the decision (at the time it was made) that he or she should enter a hospital for treatment (see Appendix A, Table A.2). When half or more of the network members who responded gave the same general response, that response was used to characterize the pre-patient's reaction. This criterion is, of course, less desirable than having the pre-patient's own reaction to the questions, but first-person reactions were impossible to obtain. Collective judgement by network members, however, is probably a valid proxy measure of pre-patient reactions.

Figure 4.2 contains a summary of network members' reports of how the pre-patient responded to being defined as mentally ill and being told that hospitalization was necessary. The first question concerned the patient's reaction to being defined as mentally ill. Networks of Vulnerable Deviants and Protected Deviants reported lower agreement from patients.

On the question of hospitalization we found a very similar pattern. Vulnerable Patients and Protected Patients had the largest proportion of networks who said that the pre-patient agreed with the decision to hospitalize. It appears that patients who have been committed for medical reasons are more likely to agree that they have a mental illness and more likely to agree that hospitalization is necessary. In contrast, patients with nonmedical symptoms are less likely

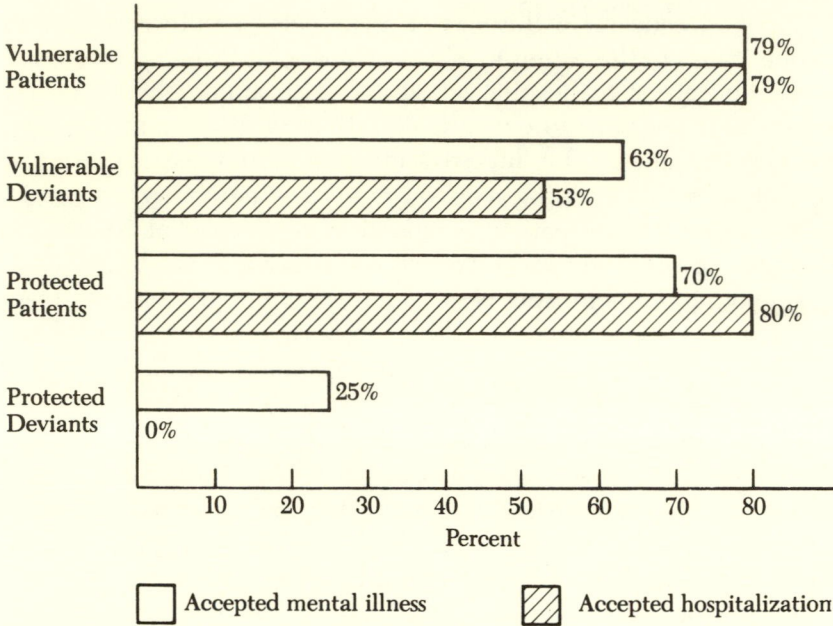

Figure 4.2 Accepted mental illness   Accepted hospitalization

Figure 4.2 Percentage of Social Networks Reporting that Patient Accepted Definition of Illness and the Need for Hospitalization.

to believe they have a mental illness for which they should be hospitalized.

Our next concern is the connection between network closeness and pre-patient reactions to the issues of illness and hospitalization. Table 4.3 contains information on the quality of emotional ties in social networks and on the reported reactions of patients to defini- tions of their problem as mental illness and to the hospitalization decision. It is clear that social networks with close emotional ties are more likely to have patients who accept their mental illness and the necessity of hospitalization. Only among Vulnerable Patients and Protected Patients (persons hospitalized for medical symptoms) was the nature of network ties related to patient reactions. Patients from Vulnerable Deviant and Protected Deviant networks did not differ in their reactions to illness and hospitalization according to the emo- tional bonds that existed among network members.

Network members were also asked if the pre-patient had sud- denly stopped doing ordinary things like working, driving, cleaning house, cooking, shopping, taking care of children, or visiting with neighbors. We summarized responses of networks across the patient

Table 4.3   Network Ties and Patients' Reactions to Their Illness and Need for Hospitalization

Patients' Reactions	Close-Tie Networks		Weak-Tie Networks	
	Number	Percentage	Number	Percentage
Patient accepts his/her mental illness	20	67%	6	35%
Patient does not accept his/her mental illness	10	33%	11	65%
Total	30		17	
Patient accepts need for hospitalization	22	73%	7	41%
Patient does not accept need for hospitalization	8	27%	10	59%
Total	30		17	

types to report the average number of activities the pre-patients stopped doing. The mean number of activities stopped for Vulnerable Patients was 2.04; for Protected Patients, 1.90; for Vulnerable Deviants, 1.54; and for Protected Deviants, 1.42. Thus, patients committed for medical symptoms stopped engaging in a somewhat greater number of activities than did patients from the other types. Nonmedical symptoms (deviant behavior) are apparently less likely to be associated with reduced activities related to work roles and household responsibilities. Medical symptoms appear to be more incapacitating to pre-patients.

Summary

In this chapter we have examined factors that appear to influence network decisions about how and when to commit a problem member. Once again we have found the most notable differences between Vulnerable Patients and Protected Patients on the one hand and Vulnerable Deviants and Protected Deviants on the other hand. The latter types exhibited total unusual behaviors that made them extremely visible to other persons. Moreover, the unusual behaviors created problems for many persons and groups involved with the pre-patients. Another important pattern was greater police involvement in the problems of Vulnerable Deviants and Protected Deviants. Finally, we have noted the substantial difference between

Protected Patients and the other patient types. Networks of Protected Patients had higher socioeconomic standing, greater knowledge of mental illness, less inclination to maintain social distance from mental patients, and more tolerance of deviance.

We also found that the decision to hospitalize was influenced by a number of contingencies and critical incidents that affected social networks. In some cases the decision to hospitalize was influenced by the existence of multiple problems in networks, which reduced their ability to continue to support members with problems. In other cases the decision was influenced by a decline in the number of members who contributed economic and psychological support to the network. The involvement of community professionals such as physicians, clergy, or legal authorities was another factor likely to lead to hospitalization. In the next chapter we turn our attention to the way in which the hospital classifies a patient who has been committed and characterizes his or her illness and family situation.

Endnotes

1. In this context we use *visible* to mean the frequency with which unusual behaviors are observed by network members. In other contexts *visible* might refer to the setting in which unusual behaviors are exhibited—that is, the public or private setting.
2. J.C. Nunnally, *Popular Conceptions of Mental Health* (New York: Holt, Rinehart and Winston, 1961).
3. The case descriptions were developed by S.A. Star, *The Public's Ideas About Mental Illness* (Chicago: National Opinion Research Center, University of Chicago, 1955). Subsequently used by B.P. Dohrenwend and E. Chin-Song, "Social Status and Attitudes toward Psychological Disorder: The Problem of Tolerance of Deviance," *American Sociological Review* 36 (1967):417–33.
4. Our procedures for defining a social network actually included some professionals as members of patients' social networks since they had continuing relationships with patients and other members prior to hospitalization. In this section professionals are referred to as "outsiders" because their relationships with pre-patients were narrow ones that concerned only the patients' problems. Their contact with pre-patients made them simultaneously members of the social networks as well as key factors in influencing commitment.
5. E. Goffman, *Asylums,* Garden City, N.Y.: Anchor Books, 1961.

Chapter 5

THE ORGANIZATIONAL RECORD: HOW HOSPITALS RESPOND TO PATIENTS AND NETWORKS

When the social network of the pre-patient decides that admission to a mental hospital is the best course of action, there is set in motion a procedure designed to officially record the event. Network members who have been discussing the pre-patient's problems among themselves, or with clergy or mental health professionals, must now formally and publicly state their reasons for seeking commitment to a mental hospital for one of their network. A member of the network, as the committing party or closest relative, must complete an Application for Investigation of Mental Health. Information provided by the committing party, along with statements of an attending physician and a diagnostic impression, are a part of what are referred to as *presenting data*. These data are the way in which the patient is "introduced" to the hospital. A sample of presenting data follows:

Q: When were the first signs of mental illness observed by you?
A: January, 1968.
Q: What were the first signs observed by you?
A: Extreme tiredness.
Q: Describe the behavior that leads you to believe this person is mentally ill.
A: Refuses to talk to anyone, including her own family.
Statement of Attending Physician: Over the past two years patient has gradually withdrawn from everything and everybody. Her affect is quite flat

and family collateral information, her husband and children, reveal that she will not converse with the family, does not do her housework, does not answer the phone, and spends most of her time just sitting. She is depressed and acts at times as if there might be some paranoia. At times she has talked in terms of self-destruction, but it has been indirect. It is my opinion that she is bordering on schizophrenia, mildly catatonic.

In cases where a voluntary admission is being sought, the presenting data are obtained from a preadmission interview with the patient and his or her parents, spouse, or some other close relative. This interview is not extensive but seeks basic information about why admission is being sought and what behavior of the pre-patient is being used to justify the request.

Basic social and demographic information (age, religion, sex, race, marital status, education, occupation, number of children) and information on the reasons for hospitalization provide the basis for creating an organizational record on the new patient. Starting out as a slim, one- or two-page entry, the record may eventually grow to be a ten-to-twelve-inch-thick file. Usually within several weeks after admission, three other major entries are added in the new patient's file. The first, the *psychological report*, is based on interview and testing procedures. This report provides the basis for a diagnostic impression. A typical psychological report follows:

> *Patient is a neat but plain looking lady of forty-two. She was cooperative with testing procedures but repeatedly expressed that she experienced some difficulty in focusing her eyes. This was probably a side effect of the medication. Patient graduated from high school but she has constant difficulty in finding words that will convey precisely the idea that she had in mind. Also, on several occasions she could not even understand the more simple instructions that she had to follow during the test. The tests do not indicate the presence of obvious psychotic disorganization even though there are many indicators that the patient is on the border of such disintegration. It seems that until this time, the patient was able to use isolation and withdrawal to protect herself against intolerable stresses. However, should she continue to maintain such an attitude of orientation in life, her contact with reality will be progressively more weakened by the increased withdrawal and her lack of insight and understanding of the environment. Interpersonal relationships will deteriorate into outright confusion and distortion and she will become an acute suicidal risk in the style of psychotic depression.*
>
> *Diagnostic Impression: Depressive neurosis, severe in an inadequate personality.*

The second major file entry is a *social history* on the patient. The history is usually obtained by a staff social worker from interviews with members of the patient's social network and with the patient. This entry includes a discussion of the patient's childhood and adolescence, school experiences, relationships with siblings and parents, and most recent situation prior to hospitalization. As with most entries in a patient's official record, the social history is very selective in the topics covered and very superficial in treatment. A ten-year period in a patient's life may be described in a single, generalized sentence ("informant stated that the patient's siblings teased her and made fun of her during her adolescence"), and no effort is made to provide any balance of information or to evaluate the quality of the information obtained.

The final major entry in the early construction of a patient's official record is the *report of the diagnostic staff*. Usually within a month after admission, the new patient is "presented" to diagnostic staff for discussion of the case by medical staff and for establishing an official diagnosis.

The official hospital record represents more than simple compliance with a bureaucratic procedure in which an administrative agency (e.g., the State Board of Mental Health) mandates that certain information must become part of a patient's hospital record. The record constitutes a definition of reality with regard to a patient and his or her social situation. How a patient is diagnosed, the strengths and problems of a patient's social network, and the moral character of a patient constitute the hospital's definition of the patient's social and psychological existence—a definition that will have continuing influence on the patient's future. Statements entered into a hospital record during the first week that concern a patient and his or her social network will reappear in the record months or even years later as if they were new observations rather than repetitions.

In this chapter we examine the *constructed reality* of a patient and his or her social network as contained in the official hospital record. Of special interest is the degree of correspondence that exists between descriptions of patients in their hospital records and in their social networks. Our aim is to determine if a relationship exists between certain characteristics of social networks and the accuracy with which network definitions of reality correspond to organizational reality. We are also interested in how the hospital record describes the social network from which the patient has come. Or-

ganizational definitions of social networks can have important consequences for a patient's chances for home visits, convalescent leave,
or early discharge.

Patients' Symptoms: Hospital and Network Perceptions

The first point of comparison between social networks and hospital
records is the question of the first unusual behaviors exhibited by
the pre-patient. In Chapter 3 we discussed how each network
member had been asked to describe the first unusual behavior of the
pre-patient that he or she had observed. The process of seeking
admission to the hospital involves answering a similar question:
"What were the first signs of mental illness observed by you?" The
hospital record contains only one response by one member of the
network—either the committing party or the closest relative involved in the commitment. However, the answers obtained from
interviews with network members may be as numerous as the
members of the network.

Figure 5.1 contains a summary of the first unusual behaviors reported in patients' hospital records. The figure also contains the
description of the first unusual behaviors observed by network
members and provided during interviews. It is clear from the figure
that hospital records of patients were far more likely to contain
allegations of "delusions and hallucinations" and "assaultive and aggressive behavior" than any other symptom category. There were
several important differences between what appeared in hospital
records and what network members said when interviewed about
the first signs of mental illness exhibited by the patient. First, in
comparison to network members' reports, hospital records tended to
overstate the existence of both the most stereotypical and the most
threatening symptoms. Delusions and hallucinations are probably
the symptoms most likely to be associated with mental illness, and to
be described as assaultive or aggressive implies greater threat of
bodily harm to other people than does any other symptom. Figure
5.1 also shows that network members tended to overstate, relative
to hospital records, symptoms such as "physical problems," "social
withdrawal," and "strange and annoying habits." It is also worth
noting that network members generally did not exhibit a high degree of agreement concerning the initial symptoms. Only twenty-

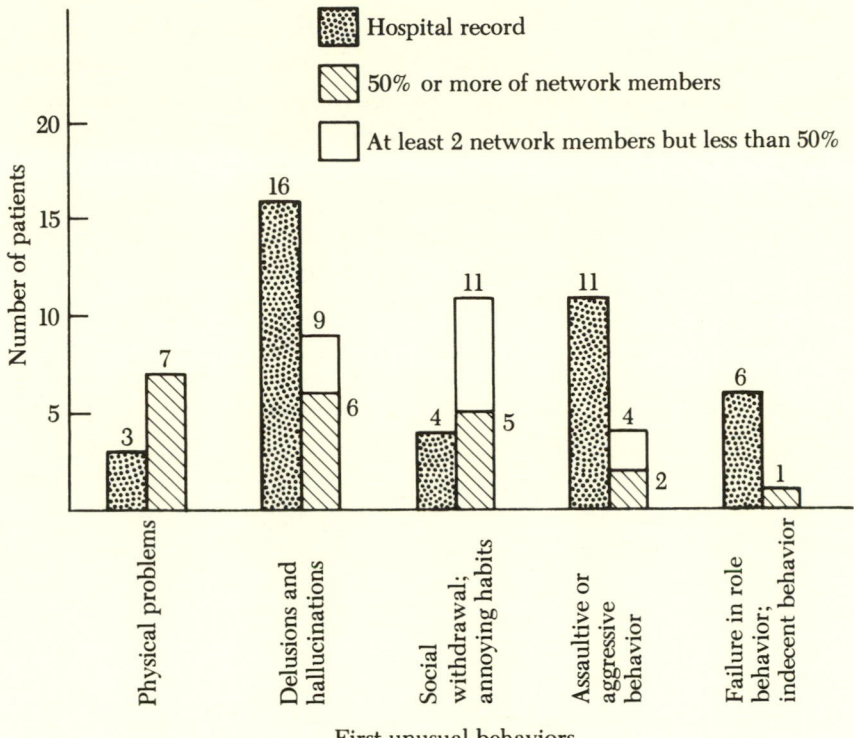

Figure 5.1 First Unusual Behaviors of Patients as Reported in Hospital Records and as Obtained from Network Members.

one of the forty-seven networks had at least half or more of their members in agreement on the initial symptoms. In thirty-two of the forty-seven networks at least two persons agreed on the initial symptoms. However, in fifteen networks each member had a different recollection of the initial symptoms.

The description of initial symptoms in the patient's hospital record contains no indication that differences of opinion might exist in regard to what the symptoms actually were. The hospital's choice of the most stereotypical and threatening symptoms for inclusion in the patient's record may be an accurate reflection of what the committing party or closest relative stated on the commitment forms or in the preadmission interview. However, the hospital record more than likely reflects a conservative bias on the part of the hospital insofar as it selects from a wide range of possible symptoms those most suited for legitimizing the commitment decision.

A comparison of hospital records and network member views on initial symptoms was also made for the four patient types (data not shown). Substantial difference between symptoms described in hospital records and reported by network members was found for three of the four patient types. Hospital records of Vulnerable Patients overstated the symptoms of "delusions and hallucinations," and records of Vulnerable Deviants overstated symptoms of "assaultive and aggressive behavior." Only Protected Patients had a pattern of symptoms described similarly in hospital records and in reports of network members.

There are several possible explanations for the discrepancies found among patient types. First, the hospital may be much more sensitive about giving accurate characterizations of the symptoms, social history, and presenting data of patients with greater social resources. Because of occupational, educational, and marital circumstances, such patients appear to occupy a somewhat higher social position and may thereby receive more consideration from hospital representatives. A second, more plausible explanation is that the social networks of Protected Patients may provide clearer and fuller information to hospital representatives, and thus a better representation of network views finds its way into hospital records. As we saw earlier, networks of Protected Patients appeared better educated, more knowledgeable about mental illness, closer in their interrelationships, and better organized to make important decisions. Such characteristics very probably manifest themselves in some way in the interactions between the hospital and the network.[1]

Basis of Network-Hospital Agreement

To better understand some of the reasons for agreement or disagreement between hospital records and statements by network members, we can examine the two extreme situations of total and nearly total agreement on the one hand, and total disagreement on the other hand. In five of the cases we examined, information on initial symptoms contained in hospital records corresponded exactly to what all network members reported. In another five cases two thirds or more of network members were in agreement with information in hospital records. These ten cases represent the extreme of total and nearly total agreement. The other extreme consists of eleven cases in which there was total disagreement between what each network member reported concerning initial unusual behavior and what was contained in hospital records. A comparison of similarities and differences between the cases of extreme agreement and extreme disagreement yielded the following results:

1. There were no differences between cases of extreme agreement and extreme disagreement on the committing symptoms or on the occupational, educational, and marital status of patients. That is, patients from the four types were found in similar proportions among the cases of agreement and of disagreement.

2. There were no differences in the size of the social network for cases of agreement and of disagreement. It was expected that, as the size of the network increased, agreement between information in records and information given by all (or almost all) network members would be increasingly difficult to attain. This finding was not supported by the data. Networks containing as many as nine members were found to be in agreement with hospital records, and networks with as few as one or two persons were found to be in total disagreement.

3. Cases of agreement between hospital and network, as compared to cases of disagreement, were more likely to involve patients who were male (50 percent versus 36 percent), older (forty-three years old versus thirty-three years old), and married (50 percent versus 18 percent). We speculate that it may be more difficult to get a married, middle-aged male committed than a young, unmarried male or female. If so, network members associated with older, married, male pre-patients must present a clearer, more consistent set of justifications for commitment if they are to be successful in convincing persons in authority to make or approve the decision. If networks speak with one voice on the pre-patients' "signs of mental illness" and the need for hospitalization, their views are more likely to be represented in hospital records.

4. The finding in regard to married, middle-aged males was supported by the finding that cases of agreement between hospital and network were more likely to involve social networks in which there was total or majority consensus on the first unusual behaviors exhibited by the pre-patient. Cases of agreement were also somewhat more likely to involve networks whose members described network relationships as "close." There was no difference between cases of agreement and disagreement in the extent to which they involved networks whose members had good lines of communication concerning the pre-patient's condition.

These findings should be approached with caution because of the small number of cases involved and the magnitude of the differences found. A shift of one or two cases would cause noteworthy changes in the magnitude of obtained percentages. Nonetheless, the findings suggest some reasons why some hospital records contain information that closely reflects network information and some do not. Hospital staff responsible for entries in a patient record may be more attentive to networks that speak more forcefully and with one voice about their pre-patients. The result would be greater agreement between the hospital record and the network. On the other hand, patients who are young, unmarried members of social networks that have fewer close ties among members and less consensus about unusual pre-patient behaviors present hospital staff with greater opportunity to ignore information coming from the network and to construct reality (i.e., the patient's record) in a way that suits the staff's own beliefs and prejudices or serves the interests of the hospital.

Legitimation of Commitment: Building a Patient's Record

Data thus far presented on initial symptoms described in a patient's hospital record indicate that the organizational record tends to select information indicating that commitment was a necessary decision. The hospital records tend to mention the most severe or serious symptoms as the first signs of mental illness exhibited by the patient. These symptoms appear in the record despite the fact that they are not mentioned with the same frequency by network members.

In addition to the presenting data from which we obtained information on initial symptoms, the hospital record also contains other information that can be viewed as supportive of the commitment, although support is not its official purpose. For example, the social history is designed to provide additional information about patients concerning their relationships with other persons and important events and experiences at different points in their lives. Often, however, the *social* history can become a *psychological* history that catalogs the different symptoms exhibited by patients at different points in their lives.

In this section we examine whether the supportive data in a patient's record tends to contain frequent mention of symptoms and thereby to continue the legitimation function of official records. If the supportive data does appear to be part of the legitimation process, we then have additional support for our hypothesis that an important purpose of the hospital record is to justify decisions rather than to store potentially useful social, medical, and psychological information on the patient.

Supportive data were examined to see how many patients were described as exhibiting one or more of eight symptoms. Figure 5.2 shows the percentage of patients whose hospital records made mention of each symptom. About 50 percent of the patients had records that mentioned three symptoms ("physical symptoms," "assaultive or aggressive behavior," and "role failures"), and approximately another 33 percent of the patients had three other symptoms noted in their records ("delusions and hallucinations," "strange and annoying behavior," and "violations of codes of decency"). Thus, rather frequent mention of symptoms was made in the social history statements contained in hospital records. These findings, in combination with the findings reported in Figure 5.1, indicate a distinct tendency for official hospital records to emphasize selective reporting of mate-

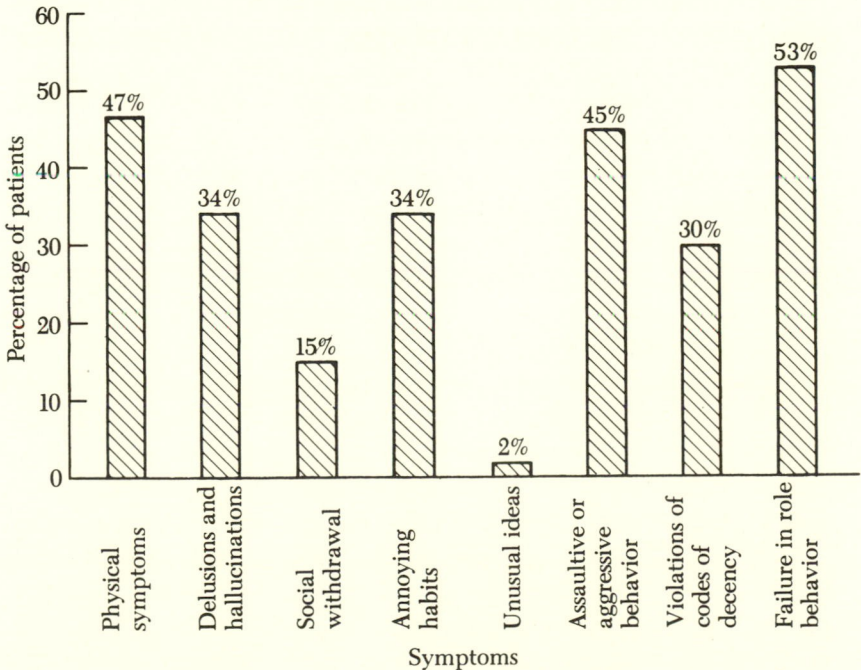

Figure 5.2 Percentage of Patients with Reported Symptoms in Their Hospital Records.

rial that would justify the commitment decision. Attention to the documentation of patients' symptoms is essential when one considers presenting data, because the data are designed to explain why commitment took place. However, supportive data do not exist for the purpose of explaining commitment but for obtaining extensive information on patients that might be helpful to the staff. Moreover, the substantial difference between what network members say about a patient and what appears in a patient's record raises further questions about how and why certain kinds of information get into the official record.

A final point about symptoms mentioned in supportive data concerns the degree of difference, if any, found among the four patient types. Vulnerable Patients, Vulnerable Deviants, and Protected Deviants had very similar patterns of symptoms mentioned in the supportive data sections of their hospital records. Each group of patients had, on the average, an additional 3 symptoms mentioned in their records. Protected Patients, on the other hand, had an average of only 1.5 additional symptoms mentioned in their hospital records (data not shown).

Once again, then, the experience of Protected Patients has been found different from other patient types. The presenting data in official records of Protected Patients contained information on symptoms that was very similar to descriptions of symptoms provided by members of the patients' social networks. In addition, the supportive data sections in their records did not serve to provide elaboration of patient problems and additional documentation of psychological symptoms. In short, the hospital records of Protected Patients did not have the character of dossiers (as compared to medical documents) that served to justify a commitment decision by selective inclusion of information.

The question of *why* the records of Protected Patients differed from those of other patients is both important and complex. Earlier we speculated that the difference might be due to selected characteristics of Protected Patients and their networks. Both the patients and their networks may confront hospital staff much more as "equals," able to engage in information exchange and able, if necessary, to make demands on the hospital. The hospital may also perceive Protected Patients and their networks as more positively oriented toward psychiatric treatment. In the hospital's view, such patients may approach hospitalization as an opportunity for treatment and recovery. That is, Protected Patients are trying to *get into* the hospital with the full support of family and friends.[2] The hospital may view other patient groups, on the other hand, as trying to *stay out of* the hospital and as having networks that are ambivalent about the need for hospitalization. Thus, only the reluctant patients require hospital records that convincingly demonstrate the need for hospitalization.

How the Hospital Views Patients' Social Networks

As we have noted, when a patient enters the hospital the staff makes an effort to bring together information about the patient in an official hospital record. The earliest and most extensive entries, the "presenting data," are designed to provide "evidence" of the existence of mental illness and justification for seeking hospitalization. The second important part of the record is the social history, which attempts to provide some understanding of important experiences and events at different stages in the patient's life. Such information is mainly descriptive and is not designed to be used in the diagnosis and prognosis for new patients.

Neither of these early entries is required by hospital procedure or by common practice to comment on or to evaluate the social networks out of which patients come. Information about networks is ordinarily obtained when patients are being considered for release (i.e., convalescent leave or discharge), at which time the social work staff attempts to describe and evaluate the setting into which patients will be released. In most cases the setting is the family from which the patient came. However, the setting may also be a residential facility such as a halfway house or nursing home where former mental patients may work and live.

Given the kind of information included in early entries in the hospital record, any staff effort to comment upon or to evaluate a patient's social network is noteworthy. A physician's report on the preadmission interview or a social worker's version of the patient's social history that goes out of the way to comment on a patient's social network may have far-reaching consequences for how a patient experiences hospital life. For example, assume that a physician or social worker makes extremely negative comments about a patient's family in early entries in the hospital record. Such comments can lead ward nurses or attendants to avoid encouraging a new patient to think about weekend leaves or the prospects of early

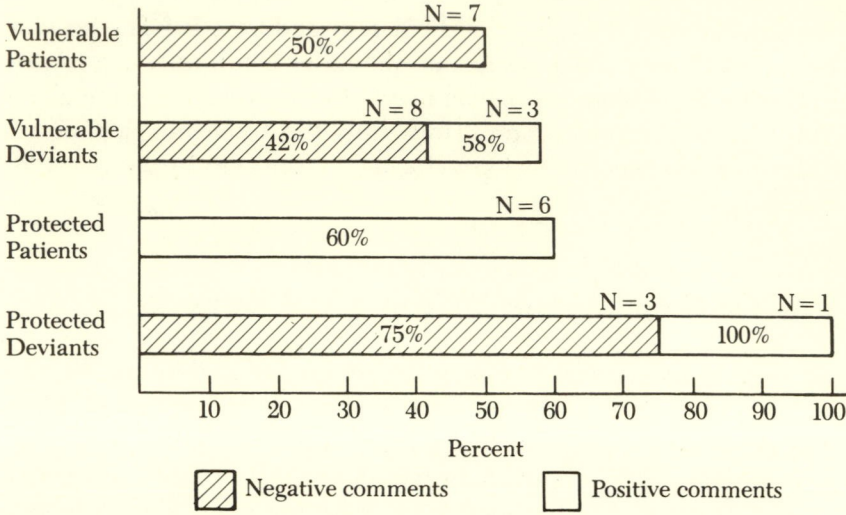

Figure 5.3 Positive and Negative Comments on Patient's Social Network Contained in Hospital Records of Four Patient Types.

release. Similarly, a ward physician who is led to view a patient's family as a nonsupportive or "pathological" social environment will not be thinking about early release or involvement of the family in the patient's rehabilitation.

Thus, positive or negative comments about a patient's social network in early entries in the hospital record can have important consequences for patients. Based upon differences noted earlier between the different types of patients and their networks, we might expect hospital records of Protected Patients to contain more positive comments about social networks than we would find in records of Vulnerable Deviants. This expectation follows from earlier findings that patients who have better social, economic, or marital resources and who belong to networks with greater knowledge of mental illness and better education come closer to reflecting middle-class family values. Thus, their networks are more likely to be evaluated as more supportive or as healthier settings.

Presenting data and social history information from all patient records were read to determine whether any mention was made of the patients' social networks. If some mention of the network was made, it was classified as either positive or negative. Figure 5.3 contains a summary of the number and kinds of comments on social networks contained in the hospital records of the four patient types.

Among Vulnerable Patients, 50 percent of their hospital records contain comments on social networks, and all comments are negative, as the following examples illustrate:

CASE 222 *Physician's admission note:* Patient is in conflict with her mother with no communication between them.

Preadmission interview: Patient said that she lives with her parents, who are drunks, which upsets her. Her mother is quite domineering and patient does not plan to stay with them.

CASE 107 Regarding [patient's] family life, his father, at the present and for quite a few years, has worked for the railroad and is away from home much of the time. When he is at home [patient's mother] states that he drinks quite a bit and becomes verbally abusive. She states that he is a very nervous man and it is very difficult for him to maintain his anxiety around the children. She further stated that his drinking has become much more heavy in the past year and he apparently has a number of problems related to his work.

CASE 431 *Preadmission interview with patient's mother:* The mother was disheveled and had been hospitalized herself in ——— in 1945. She was noted to be circumstantial and lost continuity when reporting history and had definite evidence of thought disorder.

CASE 401 Patient's mother is the only individual who works and provides some type of support. His stepfather, though appearing to be very understanding of patient's problems, has been in the clinic under the influence of alcohol and was the one that always brought patient into the clinic because he was not working. The younger brother does odd jobs and is presently unemployed and appears to be much like the patient in mentality. Mrs. ——— [patient's mother] is indifferent towards the whole thing, seems quite confused and uncertain as to her son's present condition. The whole family unit does not appear to be very healthy for someone of the patient's present state of mind. . . . Things do not seem to be conducive to good mental health at all. Practically all the family drinks and there is an indication that schizophrenic behavior may run in the context of the family.

Almost 60 percent of the records of Vulnerable Deviants contained comments on patient's social networks. Over three fourths of the comments were negative. Examples of negative comments follow:

CASE 228 Patient comes from a family full of problems. Present stepfather makes sexual advances to her, which means the home situation is very bad.

CASE 417 The home has been fraught with mental, financial, and emotional difficulties for all of ———'s [patient's] life.

CASE 240   When I talked to the husband, I found him to be a rather unusual person. He gave the impression of having a rather low IQ. He attempted to be helpful, but very little real information could be obtained from him. One got the impression that he did not really know what was going on, and one also wondered how he had been able to maintain himself and his family for all these years.

CASE 104   Mr. ——— [patient's husband] has no plans for her release because they are going to be divorced and ——— [patient] will no longer be his problem. Mrs. ——— [patient's sister] stated that she will do any-thing necessary but will not be able to accept ——— [patient] in the home because there is not enough room.

CASE 415   Patient and her husband were married for thirteen years. He gambled a lot, played cards practically every night of the week. . . . After she was released [from a general hospital] she went home. Conditions were bad because of her husband. The patient feels that her husband has been a contributing factor to her condition.

CASE 227   The home situation was found to be very dirty and unhappy. ——— [patient] had been promiscuous in the past, though it is felt that during her marriage she was not promiscuous in spite of the fact that her husband was. She only began dating other men and perhaps being promis-cuous after the divorce.

The three positive comments about social networks found in the records of Vulnerable Deviants provide a sharp contrast to the pre-dominantly negative comments:

CASE 230   ——— [patient] was extremely popular in school, very good grades, athletics (he was diving champion) and had a good family back-ground.

CASE 407   The family has always traveled widely. They traveled to Europe a few times and have seen many sights. The family is interested in the patient returning home after his hospitalization, completing school, and it is hoped that he might return soon.

CASE 414   Informant is the patient's sister, who is a schoolteacher, mar-ried, and is fairly level-headed in her understanding ———'s [patient's] welfare, but does not seem overprotective of the patient or unduly con-cerned for the patient's welfare and situation.

All four records of Protected Deviants contained comments on so-cial networks. Three of the comments were negative. The records rep-resent cases of rejecting or nonsupportive families or families with a great many problems. Excerpts from the hospital records follow:

CASE 234   We do have the patient's sister here as a patient and we have had her for a number of years. This tells us that perhaps there is something in the family background that is causing this illness and that ———'s [patient's] problems may have begun quite a long time ago. Her children are now gone from her and in ——— [another state] with her husband. Her husband wants a divorce and is not willing to help. One interested relative (her sister) seems tired of the responsibility and it is unknown as to whether she will be of much help in the future.

CASE 239   I talked to the sister-in-law of the patient, who told me she had been seeing psychiatrists for years. She saw a guy in ——— and then convinced her husband to go. So the whole family is squirrelly, says the sister-in-law, who I think is fairly right. . . . It seems that ——— [patient] had quite a few negative and bad feelings about her marriage, her husband, and probably her children. There have probably been problems throughout the whole marriage that the couple have been unable to deal with because of their personality weaknesses.

CASE 405   Patient states that her parents did not approve of the life that she was leading. She is living with an unemployed man who is the father of her expected child. She is living with an alcoholic who beat the hell out of her weekly.

For Protected Patients, 60 percent of the records contained comments on the patients' social networks. All comments were positive, and the entries were very brief and to the point. Apparently, positive comment can be conveyed with brevity, while negative remarks are more extended. Positive excerpts follow:

CASE 538   The parents were farmers and did reasonably well financially. The patient's husband is also a farmer who has continued with his success. They have lived and farmed in ——— since 1952.

CASE 105   The family wants to cooperate in any way possible to help the patient so that she can return home.

CASE 501   Mr. ——— [patient's husband] is a very neat, well-educated, and sincere individual. He has recently taken a job in ——— with the recreational and parks department. Patient and her husband moved to ———. Their home was far away from town and their friends and relatives were all left behind in ———. . . . Her family is a very staunch Catholic family.

CASE 221   It appears that Mr. and Mrs. ——— were quite interested in seeing their son get the help he needs. They were quite open and gave meaningful information. His parents will take him when released and when planning is formulated.

CASE 102   She admits that she had been sick, but was well now and saw no need for hospitalization at this time. Her reasons for this [are] "because she loves her family and her family loves her and she has a wonderful husband."

Especially noteworthy in the comments from records of Protected Patients is the fact that several of the positive comments made reference to plans for release. Such comments are remarkable because the material was drawn from preadmission interviews or social history data obtained in the early weeks of hospitalization. Such comments, forecasting release of a newly admitted patient, can structure and define the hospital experiences of the patient so that release becomes a commonly held expectation of both staff and the patient.

It is difficult to show how positive and negative comments introduced into the patient's record immediately following hospitalization directly influence the patient's hospital experience and hospital staff reactions to new patients. However, the findings are consistent with our hypothesis that Protected Patients' records contain a greater number of positive entries about social networks than do the records of any other type of patient. The most important piece of evidence in support of the view that early entries in a patient's record can produce a positive or negative self-fulfilling prophecy is found in discharge rates. Of the nineteen patients who had negative remarks about social networks in their records, only eight (42 percent) had been discharged within the first year of hospitalization. In contrast, of the ten patients who had positive remarks about social networks in their records, seven (70 percent) had been released in the first year (five of the seven were Protected Patients and the other two were Vulnerable Deviants). Thus, while entries in a patient's record cannot be viewed as the sole or most important determinant of a patient's hospital experience and chances for discharge, what is placed in a patient's record can be an important contributing factor to the career of the mental patient.

Interpreting Hospital Records: Some Conclusions

Anyone who takes the time to read lengthy patient records will be confronted with a bewildering array of information—some of it meticulously detailed and organized and some of it confusing, disorganized, and without apparent purpose. The reader will find detailed lists of a patient's personal belongings: gold-rimmed eye-glasses, false teeth, silver Bulova wristwatch, ball-point pen, one winter coat—blue, two pairs of low-heeled shoes, two print summer dresses, and so on. There will also be long and yellowing lists of prescribed medications, reports of physical exams and tests, and descriptions of the patient's condition and possessions after return-ing from a weekend home visit. The patient record is noteworthy for the relatively limited information it contains concerning the patient's social and psychological condition during the hospital stay. After the presenting data, social history, and diagnostic staff reports, which enter the patient's record in the first weeks of hospitalization, most other entries are repetitions of earlier notes or ritual recordings of irrelevant information.[3]

There would appear to be at least three different ways to interpret the meaning and purpose of the patient's hospital record. First of all, the record is a *bureaucratic document* designed to enable the hospi-tal to comply with externally imposed regulations. The State De-partment of Mental Health, hospital licensing associations, and pro-fessional medical or nursing associations may all require evidence that certain standards of care and treatment are being satisfied. Thus, the record contains careful documentation of all medication administered to the patient as well as detailed records of the pa-tient's personal possessions. From the point of view of care and treatment, such entries are part of bureaucratic ritual—that is, the entries are not used to inform hospital decisions about patient care and treatment. In short, the patient record as a bureaucratic docu-ment is externally oriented rather than patient oriented.

A second, more conventional view of the patient record is that it is a *medical record* that contains valuable information used by hospital staff in providing care and treatment. This view is difficult to support in light of the fact that very little information about patients' social and emotional conditions can be found in records beyond the early entries made in connection with admission to the hospital. The rec-ord seems designed more to restate and reaffirm what the patient was like on admission rather than to document significant changes in the patient's condition.

The most critical interpretation that can be placed on the hospital record is to view it as a *political dossier*. As such, the record is designed to justify the hospitalization decision and to legitimate the power of the state and its representatives. Information that might question the hospitalization decision or that might put the hospital in a questionable position will be selectively excluded from the dossier. What is best for the patient, or what might contribute to care, treatment, and rehabilitation, is not the primary concern of the hospital record.

Regardless of the interpretation one chooses to put upon hospital records, it is clear that many questions can be raised about what appears in the record. In particular, records contain numerous errors, contradictory information, irrelevant remarks, and unclear and potentially confusing statements. The frequency with which errors and confusing material appear suggests that records are not taken very seriously by hospital staff. Otherwise, the hospital might make greater efforts to train staff in the proper preparation of entries or to reconcile or correct existing errors.

Let us examine some questionable information from patient records. Following are examples of irrelevant remarks that either clutter records or can be potentially harmful to the patient (italics added):

CASE 107   This is an 18-year-old Negro male. Patient believes he is God, St. Peter, and Superman. He has auditory hallucinations. Has received ECT on several occasions. *He is a lazy teenage boy.*

CASE 401   Patient is oriented in all three spheres. He wants to go home right away. He is evasive, using rationalization. He admits to auditory hallucinations of his dead father's voice. *His father had never had a chance in this life, as he had diabetes, syphilis, and high blood pressure.*

CASE 420   On interview patient is clear, oriented, accessible, and in contact. Clean, but rather shabbily attired and cared for perhaps. *She wears black glasses.*

In many cases, record entries are confusing and have more than one meaning. It would be very difficult to try to take action on the basis of such entries because their validity is clearly in question, as the following examples demonstrate (italics added):

CASE 237   [Presenting data for admission—from physician's report.] Chief complaint: Patient has been masturbating since age of twenty-one. Patient claims to have been masturbating since six years ago. Also he claims to have so many pimples that he'd have to clean his face all the time. *He has halitosis and dirty feet.* Hallucinatory.

[The above note seems to imply that excessive masturbation is partly responsible for commitment. Following is a later note in the patient's records that appears to question this assumption when the patient states it to be the reason for his hospitalization.] Mr. ———— appeared slightly apprehensive and self-conscious. He showed no signs of interest or having any responsibilities. The family dates his illness to his first year in college and he has become progressively worse, with bouts of belligerence, agitation when in crowds, threats of suicide. He has had psychiatric care and institutional therapy, but now he refuses help. His speech is rambling. He thinks he was admitted for masturbating.

CASE 420 [Statement by patient's father—from Application for Investigation of Mental Health.] He claims that she's having epileptic seizures and she *has some problem with alcohol.*

[Presenting data for admission—from physician's report.] Diagnostic impression: chronic brain syndrome associated with convulsive disorder with personality disorder of passive aggressive type and *alcoholism.*

[Admission note—from hospital staff.] Patient was admitted on 8–24–71 on a temporary new admission. Father is petitioner who alleged (sic) epileptic seizures and alcoholism. The attending doctor reports *compulsive alcoholism* and epilepsy.

[From hospital social history entry.] Patient had *chronic and compulsive use of alcohol.*

[From physicians in hospital's medical clinic where patient was sent because of physical complaints.] She denies any other serious illnesses. She does not smoke. She states that she has been drinking more in the past few months, but I gather that *she has never really been an alcoholic.*

The above entries start with a statement by the committing party that the patient "has some problems with alcohol." Successive entries convert the statement into "alcoholism," "compulsive alcoholism," and "chronic and compulsive" use of alcohol. Finally, a statement by one of the medical staff questions the alcoholism label.

The best summary statement that one might offer about the hospital record is that it reveals a blatant disregard on the part of hospital staff for the *truth value* of information incorporated into it. Statements about the patient's past behavior, current symptoms, relationships with family, and so on, appear to be accepted at face value. No apparent effort is made on the part of the staff to reconcile conflicting information or to clearly identify the source of a statement. It is sometimes not possible to determine if the source of a statement is the hospital staff, the patient, or the committing party. In addition, each person who makes an entry in the record—staff physician, social worker, or ward staff member—seems to do so without considering any other entries and without any apparent concern about the integrity of the total record. In short, there is no way of assessing the quality or source of the information contained in the patient record. Thus, the hospital record, whether viewed as bureaucratic ritual, medical record, or political dossier, is composed of information of questionable validity.

Endnotes

1. Protected Deviants also had a very close correspondence between the initial symptoms described in hospital records and those reported by network members in interviews. Because of the small number of networks involved, we approach the findings cautiously. However, it is still important to note that Protected Deviants are patients with economic, educational, and marital resources comparable to those of Protected Patients. This would lead us to expect similar reactions from the hospital toward patients with higher social standing. On the other hand, the fact that networks of Protected Deviants did not show the same strengths as networks of Protected Patients limited the likelihood that hospital personnel were reacting in the same way to network members with similar social and educational characteristics.

2. The most plausible explanation for these differences is that most Protected Patients were "voluntary" admissions, while the other patient types were involuntary. There is, however, no support for this hypothesis. Only eleven of the forty-seven patients were admitted on a voluntary basis, and they were distributed in a uniform manner across the four patient types. It should also be recalled that in Chapter 1 we raised serious questions about the meanings that should be associated with voluntary admission, and about the ways, if any, voluntary admissions differ from involuntary admissions. For example, the hospital record of one "voluntary" admission stated: "She was brought in by her husband, who signed the voluntary application on her behalf, because the patient was clearly out of contact and could not sign herself."

3. On many psychiatric wards staff members (nurses and attendants) will maintain a "ward book" that contains a variety of notes about how different patients may have behaved on a particular shift. The ward book is unofficial and probably contains more useful information about how patients are getting on in the hospital than does the official record. The ward book is more convenient for staff because they have only to look at a small book to review key events from a prior shift rather than look through the ward charts of fifty patients. The ward book probably also allows staff to make entries they might not be prepared to justify or defend if the entries had the status of official notes.

Chapter 6

THE HOSPITAL EXPERIENCE: TREATMENT AND RELEASE

By the time a patient is hospitalized, the patient's network has selected from a variety of behaviors symptoms that produce a picture of a person who is either a Deviant unable to handle the problems of everyday life or a Patient with more typical psychiatric symptoms. Upon the patient's admission, the hospital staff not only records the data given by the committing network member but also records evaluations of both the patient and the committing network member. The evaluation includes appearance, resources, and descriptions of the patient's symptoms.

It is against this background that the troubled individual becomes a mental patient. It is also against this background that decisions are made about the kind of treatment a patient is to receive. The type of treatment chosen may possibly coincide with the total impression the patient's symptoms, personal resources, and social network convey rather than with a narrowly clinical judgement. For example, drugs might be the treatment of choice for patients who have been described as needing social control, having few social strengths or resources, and belonging to social networks that appear disorganized and unwilling or unable to accept them back. In contrast, other treatments, such as group or occupational therapy, might be the choice for patients who exhibit symptoms more amenable to psychiatric explanations, who have social resources, and who belong to capable and concerned social networks.

Like the kind of treatment chosen, the records kept about the patient's hospital experience may reflect the information staff members already have. Nurses, for example, may think it important to keep detailed notes as evidence of interest in patients who are relatively advantaged and who have concerned family and friends who may ask about them.

While decisions are being made in the hospital, the social network also has a chance to think through the decision it has already made and to formulate plans for how it will deal with the hospitalization. Some networks will be sure of the decision they have made. Others will begin to rethink their choice and to question whether the patient is mentally ill and belongs in a mental hospital. The way network members feel about the decision to hospitalize may affect the frequency of their visits to the patient and the number of times they take the patient home on leaves of absence. Following the hospital experience, release or abandonment is the final stage in the career of the mental patient. Whether the patient is released may be affected by all the factors that led to his or her hospitalization as well as by the hospital experience.

In this chapter we focus on the hospital experience and on the factors associated with release. In discussing the hospital experience, we look at treatment within the hospital as well as at the chance the patient has to interact with family and friends. Release or abandonment is discussed in terms of patient types and the network characteristics associated with each type. We also examine a career that might typically be associated with release and one that might result in abandonment.

The Hospital Experience

In this section we compare the hospital experiences of the four types of patients primarily as the experiences are reported in the hospital record. Our first concern is the care and attention the patient receives inside the hospital. We examine (1) the kinds and the number of different treatments received, and (2) the number of nursing notes recorded about a particular patient. Next we analyze the character of the contact between the social network and the hospitalized individual. Factors to be considered are (1) the number of visits made to the patient in the hospital, (2) the number of times the patient was taken out on leave, and (3) the number of days the patient spent outside the hospital on leave.

Kinds and Number of Treatments

Three kinds of treatment were predominant in the hospital records: drug therapy, occupational therapy, and individual or group therapy. We conceptualize drug therapy as consistent with a social control model that emphasizes custody rather than treatment. That is, drug therapy, which is designed to make patients amenable to therapy, is often used to control patients rather than to cure them. Therefore we expected to find drug therapy most prevalent among Vulnerable Deviants and least prevalent among Protected Patients. However, as Table 6.1 shows, no pattern was evident. Drug therapy was the sole treatment in only one Vulnerable Deviant case. It was most often used alone for Vulnerable Patients and Protected Deviants. The fact of overriding importance is that drugs were used in most cases, either alone or in combination with other treatments.

Another way to consider treatment is to look at the total number of different types of treatment administered to patients (see Figure 6.1). We expected that Vulnerable Deviants would receive the fewest kinds of treatment because their prognosis for recovery was poorest, their resources low, and their social networks defined as the

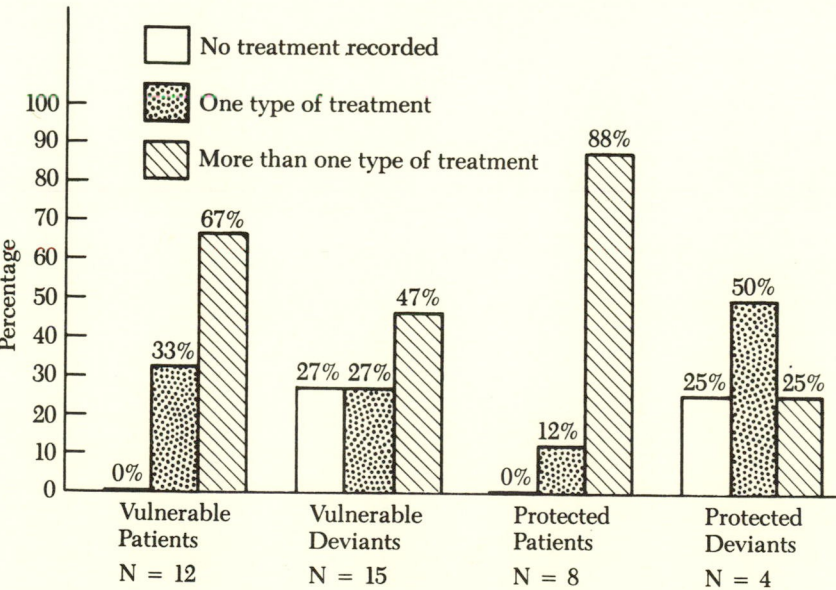

Figure 6.1 Number of Types of Treatment. (*Note:* Base is the number of patients in each patient type for whom we had hospital records.)

Table 6.1   Types of Treatment Received

Treatment	Vulnerable Patients (12)		Vulnerable Deviants (15)		Protected Patients (8)		Protected Deviants (4)	
	Number	Percentage	Number	Percentage	Number	Percentage	Number	Percentage
No record	—	—	4	27	—	—	1	25
Drugs	3	25	1	6	1	12	1	25
Occupational therapy	—	—	1	6	—	—	—	—
Drugs; individual or group therapy	—	—	1	6	2	25	1	25
Drugs; occupational therapy; individual or group therapy	8	67	6	40	5	62	—	—
Other	1	8	2	13	—	—	1	25

Note: Base is the number of patients in each patient type for whom we had hospital records.

least organized and interested. In contrast, Protected Patients would receive the most varied treatment.

The hospital records contained no treatment information for 27 percent of the Vulnerable Deviants and for 25 percent of the Protected Deviants. These percentages were in sharp contrast to the figures for the Protected Patients and Vulnerable Patients. All the records for individuals in these categories contained treatment information. There are two possible interpretations for the difference. First, patients with medical-psychiatric symptoms and concerned networks were more likely than patients with deviant symptoms and disorganized networks to receive treatment while in the hospital. Second, treatment may have been given in a more uniform manner but not recorded. Either explanation is consistent with our prediction that hospital staff will evaluate patients in such a way that some are deemed more worthy of treatment and attention than are others.

Looking at the percentages of each patient type that received more than one type of treatment, we find a similar contrast. Only 47 percent of the Vulnerable Deviants and 25 percent of the Protected Deviants received more than one type of treatment, whereas 88 percent of the Protected Patients and 67 percent of the Vulnerable Patients were so treated. Patients who received only one of the common types of treatment usually received drug therapy. Only in a single case did an individual receive another common option, occupational therapy, as the sole treatment.

Nursing Notes

Nursing notes represent what nursing personnel have observed about hospitalized individuals as well as what information nurses consider important to record about a particular patient. The notes typically contain information about whether the patient's behavior is problematic, evaluations of the patient's progress, and notations that the patient has returned from a leave. However, many hospital records contain no nursing notes, and those records with notes vary as to the number, frequency, combination, and quality. Following are two examples of very different nursing notes. The first set of notes is taken from a total of forty-four separate entries about a Vulnerable Patient. The notes are short and quite repetitive. They appear to relate to whether the patient is a problem on the ward. No mention is made of the patient's having gone on leaves of absence. Also, although the patient did have an interested relative, the hospital records contain negative comments on this network member. (However, the patient was eventually released to her.)

CASE 209   9-2: Miss B——— is a new admission. Very quiet and cooperative. Rested well during the night. Patient appears to be very quiet. She socializes well with other patients. Already she seems to adjust well to the ward.

9-3: Patient quiet and cooperative and went to lab and was X-rayed this A.M. [Later] Patient has been very quiet on this shift. No behavioral problem.

9-4: Quiet and cooperative this shift. No complaints. Vital signs taken and recorded.

9-5: Patient quiet and cooperative on this shift. [Later] Patient is no problem on this shift. [Even later] Patient very quiet and cooperative. Socializes well with other patients.

9-6: Patient quiet and cooperative.

9-7: Patient appears to be quiet and cooperative at this time.

9-7: Patient appears to be quiet and cooperative at this time.

9-7: Patient wanted to wash tables, stating that she was doing nothing. She asked for a task.

10-15: Patient very quiet and withdrawn. However, patient will talk with only a few patients on ward and only to aides when spoken to. Appears very nervous and unsure of self.

The second set of nursing notes is taken from a total of fifty-five separate entries. They are long narratives and contain much detail. They indicate that the patient has been on leave and relate problematic and cooperative behavior. No solutions are given for problematic behavior and no indication is given of the importance of the information noted.

CASE 227   3-12: A 24-year-old, white female ambulatory was admitted by family as a voluntary commitment. Appears to be oriented in all the spheres. Cooperative with admission procedures. Body fairly clean. Stated that she has to get home to her children . . . "I miss them so very much." "I have many problems besides my ex-husband," she says. Appears to be adjusted to the ward fairly well.

3-13: Appears friendly and cooperative.

3-23: No complaints. Found several job openings in the paper and would like to go see about them. Stated that she could live with her boyfriend but needs a job before she can leave here.

4-7: L——— has an industrial therapy assignment. . . . She will attend this assignment. L——— is very helpful on the ward and with the ward routine and whatever else needs [to be] done. She stated that she is now beginning to realize that her husband doesn't want her and the sooner she forgets about him, the sooner she can leave the hospital, because she thinks that this is the largest part of the problem. She participates in our group freely.

4-27: She was bitten on the right hand around the wrist by ——— [another patient]. Patient told ——— [other patient] that if she ever called her names again or bit her, she would slap her down good.

5-7: Returned home from her pass easily. Sister was not very happy about how the visit went. L——— feels she should be able to do what she wants, when she wants and have her boyfriend spend the night, if she so desires. Her boyfriend is now in Kentucky. The sister doesn't want the worry of her staying in Valparaiso with the boyfriend. She feels she is going to be able to just walk out of here with no place to go and do what she wants. She stated she wanted sister to bring her some aspirin. I explained that she couldn't have them on the ward, that she gets medications out of the office with an order. She stated, "Well, I can have them if the doctor says." Sister stated she could call in for another pass but didn't sound too happy. She is afraid she is going to get into trouble. Told sister that she got some cigarettes from the store and had really taken them from sister's house. She told the sister that she should be happy that she stole from her and not the store. . . . She could have done that. She seems very hyperactive, sort of smart alecky and sassy, and doesn't care to listen to anybody. Refused to take her medications while home, but this medication was discontinued before the pass anyway.

5-11: She is very lazy but also very helpful when asked to do something . . . she will usually do it. Sister put in for several passes but did not come to pick her up. She's neat and clean in her personal appearance. She has been referred to a home for unwed mothers.

A difference across patient types in the number of nursing notes may reflect either a difference in the amount of attention given to a patient or a difference in the care taken in recording what has been noticed. In either case, we expected that the records of Protected Patients would be the most complete, while those of Vulnerable Deviants would be the least complete. As Table 6.2 shows, the pattern was not stark. However, Protected Patients had the fewest records containing no nursing notes and the largest percentage of case records with 21 or more notes. The quality of the nursing notes or the kinds of information in them did not seem to vary with patient type (data not shown).

Evaluating the Decision to Hospitalize

Networks were asked to evaluate the difficulty of the decision-making process regarding hospitalization of one of their members.

Table 6.2   Number of Nursing Notes

Notes	Vulnerable Patients (12)		Vulnerable Deviants (15)		Protected Patients (8)		Protected Deviants (4)	
	N	%	N	%	N	%	N	%
None	3	25	3	20	1	12	2	50
1–20	5	42	5	33	2	25	2	50
More than 21	4	33	7	47	5	62	—	—

Note: Base is the number of patients in each patient type for whom we had hospital records.

They were also asked if they had second thoughts about their decision. Their answers bear upon their willingness to accept the patient at home again and therefore upon the likelihood of release. Let us look at network members' answers to see if they reinforce what we have already discerned about the patients, their social networks, and the decision-making process.

The first question asked was, "Would you say the decision to commit the patient to a mental hospital was a difficult one for the family to make?" A positive answer was the majority consensus answer in thirty of the forty-seven networks. Only three networks were able to give a clear "no" to the question. Five of the networks gave a majority consensus answer of "don't know." Nine of the forty-seven networks had a division among members between two or more of the "yes," "no," and "don't know" responses. Patient types showed differences in the percentage of networks that asserted that the hospitalization decision was difficult. The networks of both types of Patients were more likely to define the decision as difficult than were the networks of Deviants. Seventy-eight percent of the Vulnerable Patients and 70 percent of the Protected Patients described difficulty in making the decision. In contrast, only 53 percent of the Vulnerable Deviants and 50 percent of the Protected Deviants reported the decision as difficult.

Given the difference between patient types in the percentage of networks that found the commitment decision difficult or were uncertain about its difficulty, we examined network answers to another question, one that related to the difficulty of living with the decision that had been made. Members were asked, "Have you or any other person had any second thoughts about whether it was the right decision?" Overall, most networks had a majority of members with no second thoughts about having committed the patient to the mental hospital; thirty-nine of the forty-seven networks gave a majority answer of "no." Thus, once having made the decision, despite whether it was defined as difficult, members of organized and disorganized networks alike appeared to have accepted the decision.

Visitors and Home Visits

In addition to the treatment given and attention paid to the patient by hospital personnel, and in addition to the network's evaluation of the hospitalization decision, the patient's continued interaction with the social network has important implications for the patient's career. Such interaction is an indicator of whether members of the network have abandoned the patient or whether they still define the patient as a member of the network and expect him or her eventually to return home. We expected that networks of Vulnerable Deviants, which see the hospital as a place to control the patient, would maintain minimal contact, while networks of Protected Patients, which see the hospital as a treatment center, would maintain regular contact. We examined three measures of continued interaction: (1) the number of visits paid to the patient, (2) the number of times the patient went on leave of absence from the hospital, and (3) the number of days the patient was out of the hospital on leave.

The percentage of patients in any category who received visitors ranged from 25 to 50 percent. Surprisingly, similar percentages—approximately 25 percent—of Vulnerable Deviants, Protected Patients, and Vulnerable Patients received visitors. An even higher proportion—50 percent—of Protected Deviants received visitors.

Perhaps the issue of whether the patient leaves the hospital for visits home is a clearer indicator of the way in which networks conceptualize their hospitalized members. If so, we should find fewer patients in the Vulnerable Deviant category out on leave, and Protected Patients should be most likely to have made visits home. Again, however, the results did not correspond with what we have learned about patients and their social networks. A large percentage of all patients left the hospital on leaves of absence. Individuals in the Protected Deviant and Vulnerable Deviant categories were the most likely to have ever gone home on leave. One hundred percent of the former and 93 percent of the latter were taken home temporarily. Less likely to have been taken out on leave were individuals in the Vulnerable Patient and Protected Patient categories. Eighty-three and 75 percent, respectively, were taken home on leave.

More information can be gained from looking at the number of times an individual left the hospital (see Figure 6.2). The number of times out of the hospital ranged from one to fourteen. The Vulnerable Deviants were the most likely to leave the hospital for a moderate number of visits (one to six). Eighty percent of these individuals left the hospital between one and six times. The Protected Patients and Protected Deviants were the most likely to leave the hospital for a greater number of visits. Thirty-eight percent of the Protected Patients and 50 percent of the Protected Deviants went home between seven and fourteen times. The total number of days out of the hospital varied from a few days to over ninety days (see Table 6.3). Of the Vulnerable Deviants, 60 percent spent a total of sixty days or less out of the hospital. Thirty-two percent of the same group spent more than sixty days on leave. The six Vulnerable Deviants who were out of the hospital for thirty days or less were on leave for periods at the shorter end of the category (between one and fifteen days). In comparison, Protected Patients were more likely to stay out of the hospital for longer periods of time. Fifty percent of this

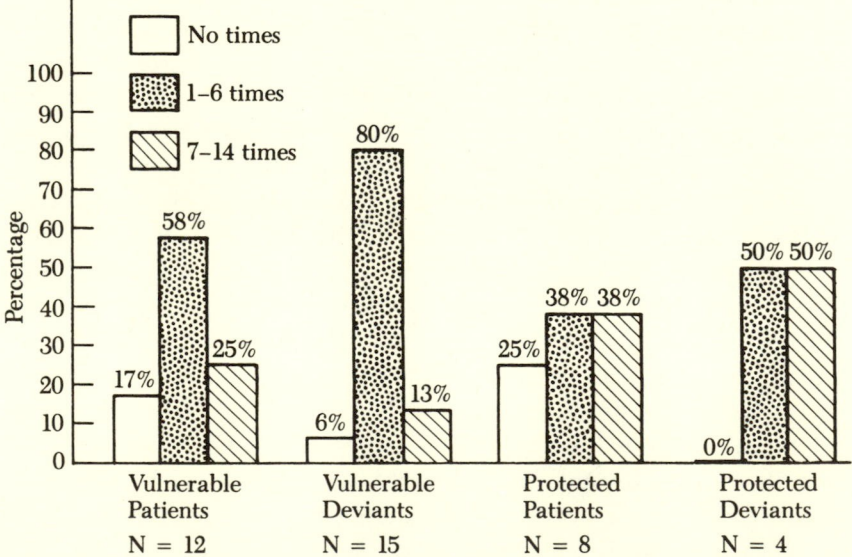

Figure 6.2   Number of Times Out of the Hospital. (*Note:* Base is the number of patients in each patient type for whom we had hospital records.)

Table 6.3 **Number of Days on Leave**

Days	Vulnerable Patients (12)		Vulnerable Deviants (15)		Protected Patients (8)		Protected Deviants (4)	
	N	%	N	%	N	%	N	%
None	2	17	1	6	2	25	—	—
1–30	5	42	6	40	1	12	2	50
31–60	2	17	3	20	—	—	1	25
61–90	3	25	1	6	2	25	1	25
90 and over	—	—	4	26	2	25	—	—
No indication of days on leave					1	12		

Note: Base is the number of patients in each patient type for whom we had hospital records.

group spent more than sixty days out of the hospital. Considering all four groups, then, Protected Patients again exhibited a distinct pattern. Protected Patients spent more time out of the hospital than did patients from other groups.

Visits with friends and relatives inside the hospital were relatively uncommon among all the patient types. In contrast, leaves of absence were a likely occurrence. Surprisingly, in comparing those who had left the hospital at least once, we found that Deviants were more likely than Patients to have ever been on leave. However, Vulnerable Deviants were more likely to have left for a moderate number of visits (one to six), while Protected Patients were more likely to have been home several times (seven to fourteen). Protected Patients spent more time out of the hospital than did any of the other three groups. The networks of Vulnerable Deviants did not seem at this time to have abandoned their members, at least in terms of continued contact. They, like other networks, visited the hospital rarely and were able to have the patient home for only for a few visits and for shorter periods of time. In contrast, networks of Protected Patients, while they did not visit much with the patient in the hospital, brought the patient home often and for long periods of time. They appeared to be preparing for the time when they would bring the patient home on a more permanent basis.

Summary of the Hospital Experience

We have followed four sets of patients into the hospital and found that differences between them persisted even after hospitalization.

There was more information in the hospital records about the number and kinds of treatment received by Patients (Protected and Vulnerable) than there was for Deviants. The available information suggested that Patients received more varied treatment. Records kept in the form of nursing notes were also more complete for Protected Patients. Although differences did appear in the content and length of nursing notes, the differences did not seem to be related to patient types.

The period immediately following hospitalization can be a time for a network to reflect on the soundness of the decision. Second thoughts on the part of network members may have some bearing on whether a network remains in contact with the patient. However, most of the networks examined (thirty-nine of forty-seven) had no second thoughts.

There were similarities and differences among patient types in relation to the length of time they spent visiting with family and friends. The percentage of patients who had visitors in the hospital was low. More patients left on leaves of absence. Protected Patients went on the largest number of leaves and were out of the hospital for the longest stretches of time.

Release or Continued Hospitalization

A career approach to understanding mental illness takes us to the final stage, which involves release or continued hospitalization. In this section we establish two model career paths to the mental hospital, each followed to a greater or lesser extent by two of our patient types. We then determine which patients were released and which remained in the hospital. We expect the data to show that differences among networks during the commitment process are closely related to whether a network is willing to have the patient back from the hospital. We focus on patient types and on selected network characteristics to answer some remaining questions about who is likely to be released.

Two Career Paths

At each stage of the career of the mental patient, we have made comparisons among patient types and the networks that surround them. Differences were most often noted between Patients and

Deviants. Similarities were most often noted between Protected Patients and Vulnerable Patients, and to a lesser extent between Vulnerable Deviants and Protected Deviants. Thus, although we have described four patient types, the information presented so far indicates that there are two paths to the mental hospital. One path involves patients who are embedded in close social networks that can be effectively mobilized by a leader and decisionmaker. These networks describe initial unusual behaviors in psychiatric terms. Although they indicate a high tolerance for deviance, they act to hospitalize the pre-patient in a relatively short period of time. Network members describe only a limited number of troublesome behaviors, both medical and nonmedical, which do not cause a great deal of trouble for neighbors and police. After hospitalization, the networks maintain extensive contact with the patient and take him or her out for numerous leaves. Based on this information, we would expect this path, which most closely fits Protected Patients and Vulnerable Patients, to end in release.

The second path involves patients who are surrounded by social networks whose members are not emotionally close to one another and who do not agree on who is the leader or decisionmaker. These networks try to normalize initial unusual behaviors by describing them in everyday language and as something other than a psychiatric problem. They take a relatively long time to act to hospitalize the pre-patient, although they indicate a low tolerance for deviance. In addition to the initial problem behavior, network members describe a long list of unusual behaviors, most of them nonmedical, which cause a great deal of disruption in the lives of others. After hospitalization, network members maintain limited contact with the patient and take him or her out on infrequent leaves. Based on this information, we would expect this path, which most closely fits Vulnerable Deviants, to end in abandonment.

Career Paths and Patient Types

At the conclusion of our study, twenty-eight patients had been discharged; nineteen patients remained in the hospital. The expectation that Protected Patients and Vulnerable Patients would be more likely to be released than Vulnerable Deviants and Protected Deviants was strongly borne out by the data. Eight of ten Protected Patients (80 percent) had been released, as had eleven of fourteen Vulnerable Patients (79 percent). In contrast, eleven of nineteen

Table 6.4 Length of Hospitalization for Discharged and Nondischarged Patients by Patient Type

Patient Status	Months Elapsed since Admission									
	1–3		4–6		7–9		10–12		13+	
	Number	Percentage	Number	Percentage	Number	Percentage	Number	Percentage	Number	Percentage
Vulnerable Patients										
discharged (11)	1	9	5	45	4	36	—	—	1	9
nondischarged (3)	—	—	—	—	1	33	1	33	1	33
Vulnerable Deviants										
discharged (8)	3	38	1	12	1	12	1	12	2	25
nondischarged (11)	—	—	—	—	—	—	5	45	6	55
Protected Patients										
discharged (8)	2	25	1	12	1	12	2	25	2	25
nondischarged (2)	—	—	—	—	1	50	1	50	—	—
Protected Deviants										
discharged (1)	1	100	—	—	—	—	—	—	—	—
nondischarged (3)	—	—	—	—	—	—	3	100	—	—

Vulnerable Deviants (58 percent) and three of four Protected Deviants (75 percent) were still in the hospital.

Before we examine the release information further, we must consider the possibility that discharge is an artifact of when patients were admitted. Let us look at months elapsed since admission for both discharged and nondischarged patients. Fifty percent of the discharged patients spent six months or less in the hospital. All of the patients not yet discharged at the conclusion of the study had already spent more than six months in the hospital. Sixty-four percent of the nondischarged patients had been hospitalized for between seven months and one year. The discharged patients had thus spent less total time in the hospital than patients who were not discharged when our study ended. Clearly, time spent as a patient is not directly related to patient status.

We have seen that a larger percentage of Patients than Deviants were released. Also, we have seen that release does not seem to be simply the result of the length of stay in the hospital. Next we look at the length of stay for discharged and nondischarged patients within types and make some comparisons across types. Table 6.4 shows that most discharged patients had been hospitalized one year or less. There was some variation across patient types. Discharged Vulnerable Patients spent the shortest time in the hospital. Surprisingly, there was not much difference between the length of time discharged Patients and discharged Deviants spent in the hospital. There were interesting similarities and differences between the patient types in regard to the length of time already spent in the hospital for nondischarged patients. All the nondischarged patients had been in the hospital at least seven months. The nondischarged Vulnerable Deviants had been hospitalized longest. Six (over 50 percent) of these patients were still in the hospital one year after commitment. Only one other patient, a Vulnerable Patient, had been in the hospital that long. The Vulnerable Deviants and Protected Deviants hospitalized for one year or less had all been in the hospital for at least ten months.

Networks' Fear of Violence

Earlier we summarized some network characteristics (e.g., closeness, agreement on a decisionmaker) associated with hospitalization and release or with continued hospitalization. However, we have not yet discussed one factor affecting a network's willingness to accept a patient back. The fears of network members that released patients might harm themselves or others are likely to be associated with discharge. Overall, most networks indicated that patients were unlikely to harm themselves or others. Twenty-five of the forty-seven networks reported that they did not fear violence on the part of the patient. Twelve networks reported a fear of violence, while nine were unsure. There was, however, a substantial difference among patient types on this variable. Among networks of Protected Patients, seven of ten (70 percent) had a majority consensus that violence was unlikely. Ten of fourteen networks of Vulnerable Patients also saw violence as unlikely. In stark contrast, ten of nineteen (over 50 percent) of the networks surrounding the Vulnerable Deviants agreed that violence was likely. In fact, ten of the twelve networks that viewed violence as likely were associated with Vulnerable Deviants. (The Protected Deviants presented a somewhat different picture, with only one of four networks afraid violence would occur.)

How does the fear that patients will harm themselves or others relate to whether or not patients are discharged? Overall, of the twenty-five patients whose networks saw violence as unlikely, seventeen were discharged and eight were not discharged. Of the twelve networks who saw violence as likely, six were discharged while six remained in the hospital. Of the nine patients whose networks were unsure about the potential for violence, five were discharged and four remained hospitalized. Across patient types, the relationship between the fear of violence and the discharge status of patients yields some interesting information. Among Patients, both Vulnerable and Protected, release was positively associated with an assessment that violence was unlikely. The ratio of released to non-released Vulnerable Patients and Protected Patients whose networks rated violence as unlikely was four to one and six to one, respectively. Among Vulnerable Deviants the pattern was different. The ratio of discharged to nondischarged patients was two to three for networks who rated violence as unlikely *and* for networks who rated violence as likely. Although the numbers were small, Protected Deviants whose networks saw violence as unlikely had a ratio of one to two of discharged to nondischarged patients.

We would expect that networks with a majority consensus that violence was unlikely should contain a higher number of released patients than nonreleased patients. The prediction was true for Vulnerable Patients and Protected Patients. In addition, the reverse should be true for networks who saw violence as likely. That is, the percentage of discharged patients among networks who saw violence as likely should be smaller than the percentage of nondischarged patients. In this case, however, the Vulnerable Deviants presented an illogical pattern. Although these networks were more prone to fear violence, the percentage of patients discharged was the same whether the network saw violence as likely or unlikely. This lack of relationship may reflect the more disorganized character of the networks surrounding Vulnerable Deviants, especially as compared to Patients' networks. Alternatively, the data may reflect the fact that the presence or absence of violence is not a factor in the willingness of these networks to accept the patient home after release.

Patient Types and Career Paths: Conclusions

Taking into account what we knew about the patient types and their surrounding networks, we expected that the career paths of Protected Patients and Vulnerable Patients would end in release, while the career paths of Protected Deviants and Vulnerable Deviants would not end in release. This expectation was strongly confirmed in terms of the Patients, approximately 80 percent of whom were discharged. The Deviants were more likely than not to remain in the hospital, and thus they also confirmed our expectation. However, the Deviants, especially the Vulnerable Deviants, presented a more mixed picture; eight of the nineteen (42 percent) were discharged. One possibility is that characteristics associated with Patients, and thus with discharge, are also associated with discharge among Deviants. Let us look at four network characteristics—ties to patient, presence of a decisionmaker, network closeness, and social distance—to see if they are associated with discharge among Deviants.

Eight of the Vulnerable Deviants had a network member close to the patient. This characteristic was not associated with discharge. Three patients with a close network member were discharged; five were not. Eleven (58 percent) of the networks of Vulnerable Deviants had a majority consensus on a decisionmaker. However, four of these patients were discharged, seven were not. A close network is another variable associated with Patients and thus with discharge. Seven of nineteen Vulnerable Deviants came from networks with strong emotional bonds. Three of these patients were discharged; four were not. Finally, social distance is a variable directly related to discharge consideration. Those networks which indicated low social distance, or a willingness to interact with former mental patients, should in theory be more compatible with receiving a patient home. Eight of the nineteen networks involving Vulnerable Deviants had low social distance scores, and their patients were evenly divided between those who were still hospitalized and those who were not. Therefore, characteristics associated with networks of Protected Patients and Vulnerable Patients, and thus with a career path that ends in discharge, were not clearly associated with release for Vulnerable Deviants. We have been able to establish a general logic for this career path but have not been able to explain why a minority—but a relatively large minority—did not follow the logic. The volatile situation of the networks of Vulnerable Deviants apparently does not lend itself to clear results.

In summary, we have found that the career path usually associated with Protected Patients and Vulnerable Patients commonly ends in release. We have also found that the career path associated with Vulnerable Deviants and Protected Deviants is less likely to end in release. Among the nondischarged patients, Deviants have spent a longer time in the hospital. Absence of fear that the patient will be violent if released is related to release among Patients but not among Vulnerable Deviants. In looking at some characteristics of the networks of discharged Vulnerable Deviants that might explain why the patients were discharged, we have found that variables such as ties to the patient, network closeness, presence of a decisionmaker, and social distance were not associated with discharge.

Two Case Histories

To conclude the chapter let us examine in some detail the career paths of two patients who were mentioned in Chapter 4 as members of multiproblem networks. The first case illustrates the career path characteristic of a Patient:

CASE 412   The patient is a 54-year-old, married, employed male who was separated from his wife and living in a motel at the time of commitment. He has two older children who live in Chicago and one 10-year-old son still at home. Other members of the network include a couple, neighbors and friends, and a minister who is also a neighbor. The wife and neighbors were interviewed. The family is not close, but there was a good deal of supportive interaction among the neighbors and family that involved both the patient and his wife. The patient was never easy to live with, according to the wife. He had hit her on several occasions. However, it was after she filed for divorce, when he began to bother others, that people began to define his bizarre behavior in terms of mental illness. His wife's report of his strange behavior while living in the motel is included in Chapter 4. The neighbors report that the patient thought (apparently incorrectly) that his wife was having an affair with an insurance man and the lovers were trying to kill him.

Shortly before committal, the husband bothered the minister in the middle of the night with stories about the patient's wife and the insurance agent. Soon afterward he called the insurance agent and was talking incoherently. The wife became afraid to let her husband take the son out on a visit. The police were called and convinced him to leave.

The wife consulted with the neighbors, the family doctor, and the husband's priest. The patient was committed shortly afterward.

In the hospital the patient received three kinds of treatment: drugs, group therapy, and activity therapy. The hospital record is lengthy and includes thirteen nursing notes. Two leaves were recorded. There was some fear of violence. *The patient was discharged and is again living with his wife.*

The second case history illustrates the career path characteristic of a Deviant:

CASE 228   The patient is a 21-year-old, single, unemployed female who was living at home with her mother, stepfather, and siblings at the time of the commitment. A friend and two aunts were part of the network. The family was not close. The problem behavior began about three years before hospitalization. The mother's extensive description includes an incident from ten years earlier. The behavior included drug use, sexual promiscuity or acting out, and suicide attempts. In addition, there is an indication from the mother and one aunt that the stepfather had made sexual advances toward the patient.

The patient's behavior was causing difficulty for the family. One aunt describes the family situation in these terms: "It was unhealthy. You could see the problems happening in the other three children." The police were also involved. The patient seemed to wander down to the police station when she became depressed.

The patient was seeing a psychiatrist, and a social worker was also involved, but the problems seemed to increase. The family, especially the mother, was unable to cope. She states: "After three years of this, we were falling apart." However, the mother, who is described as the decision-maker, says she did not commit her daughter to the hospital earlier because "I think of [the mental hospital] as a place to be dreaded and I didn't want to send my daughter there if at all possible."

The precipitating incident is described as occurring when the patient went with three young men to their apartment and subsequently accused one of them of raping her. She then decided to commit herself, and her mother agreed with the decision.

The social control aspect of the decision for the mother is clear in the following statement: "If she was doing the things that she did in the last half year, I would have seen my daughter become a prostitute. *I feel by hospitalization she hasn't got the opportunity to run around with any man that comes along*" (italics added).

The hospital records are extremely brief. The only treatment listed is drugs. There are no nursing notes. The patient has been out on leave, signed out by her mother. *The patient is still hospitalized.*

These two histories underline the importance of a career perspective to an understanding of mental illness. They indicate that career stages, although we have discussed them separately throughout the book, are interrelated in the actual experiences of networks.

Chapter 7

SOCIAL NETWORKS
AND THE CAREER
OF THE MENTAL PATIENT:
SUMMARY AND CONCLUSIONS

We began this book with a critical examination of the two most influential prevailing approaches to understanding how persons become hospitalized for mental illness. The medical-psychiatric perspective uses a disease approach that places great emphasis on the symptoms exhibited by the mentally ill. The societal reaction perspective places its emphasis on individual status resources acquired through marriage, employment, and education that influence the hospitalization decision. Each approach has made important contributions to our understanding of how people become mental patients, but both approaches are limited by theoretical views and methodology.

In the hope of answering some of the questions about how people become mental patients, we have proposed a somewhat radical departure in thinking about such questions. We have suggested, in effect, that much may be learned about the process of becoming a mental patient if we turn our attention away from the patient and toward the social networks in which the patient is embedded. Rather than being concerned with symptoms that may be responsible for hospitalization or with a patient's status resources that may influence the decision to hospitalize, we have suggested that both symptoms and resources must be examined from the point of view of the social networks that give meaning to them. It is within social networks composed of family, friends, neighbors, and co-workers that problem behaviors become defined as symptoms or a person's occupational or marital status becomes viewed as a barrier to hospitalization.

We have also suggested that serious attention must be given to the career of the mental patient as a sequence of interrelated stages through which persons move on their way to hospitalization. In so doing, we hoped to illuminate not only how social networks identify persons as having mental illness but how networks contribute to the decision to hospitalize, how they are involved in a patient's experience in the hospital, and how they influence a patient's chances of being released.

In order to determine the significance of social networks at different points in a patient's career, we used an approach that would allow us to also consider alternative and competing theoretical views. The hospitalized patients studied in this book were classified according to the kind of symptoms for which they were hospitalized and according to their individual status resources. Patients with few occupational, marital, and educational resources were considered "vulnerable," while those with more resources were considered "protected." Persons hospitalized for unambiguous medical or psychiatric symptoms were classified as "Patients," while those who violated group standards of conduct were called "Deviants." The result was four types of patients: Vulnerable Patients, Vulnerable Deviants, Protected Patients, and Protected Deviants. We viewed these types as rough approximations of key features of the medical-psychiatric and societal reaction approaches to mental illness. Protected Patients and Vulnerable Deviants were considered as pure types with consistent characteristics.

Findings

Throughout our analysis of data related to different stages in the patient career, it was possible to assess the relative importance of the patient types and the social networks associated with patients. In this way we anticipated that the significance of a social network approach would be demonstrated. The following sections summarize our findings.

Identifying and Reacting to Initial Unusual Behaviors

The career of the mental patient begins with the first incident of behavior that others respond to as "unusual." All network members were asked to describe the first unusual behavior they had observed the patient exhibit. Members were asked to describe the "what-where-when" of the behavior and their response to it in terms of perceived seriousness. They were also asked whether the behavior prompted them to take any action.

Examination of initial unusual behaviors indicated substantial variation in the behaviors exhibited and in responses to the behaviors. The responses of greatest concern to our analysis involved the ways in which social networks described initial unusual behaviors and the kind of actions they initiated in response. The data revealed a tendency for some networks to "medicalize" initial unusual behaviors and for others to "normalize" the behaviors. There were also distinct differences in the ways networks reacted to initial unusual behaviors. Some networks acted quickly to seek medical assistance and hospitalization, and others delayed such action for years.

A comparison of initial unusual behaviors across the four patient types indicated that neither the severity of the committing symptoms nor the status resources of patients accounted for the different definitions attached to unusual behaviors or to the actions that followed. Rather, the different properties of social networks are what enable us best to understand reactions to patients. Networks with positive social-emotional bonds, extensive interaction among members, and instrumental role structures responded to initial unusual behaviors by defining them in medical or psychiatric terms and taking action to bring the deviant in contact with a medical professional. Networks lacking close, supportive ties and instrumental role structures were more inclined to try to make sense of the deviance by placing it in a context of understandable behavior. The result was to "normalize" the deviance and to take no action to deal with the problem.

Deciding to Hospitalize

After the network has observed, defined, and reacted to initial unusual behaviors, the next significant stage in the patient's career occurs when the network makes the decision to hospitalize. Since all the patients in our study were hospitalized, the question that concerned us was why and how the decision was made. Why, for example, did a network finally decide to hospitalize after years of learning to live with the problem member? What circumstances affecting the network appeared to influence hospitalization? Did the nature of the hospitalization decision have a continuing influence on the patient's career, especially on the chances of release from the hospital?

Patients committed relatively soon after their unusual behaviors were observed were those whose networks focused on the medical or psychiatric character of their symptoms (Vulnerable Patients and Protected Patients). The networks associated with patients with medical or psychiatric symptoms had higher socioeconomic standing, more favorable attitudes toward the mentally ill, greater knowledge of mental illness, and greater tolerance for deviance.

Patients hospitalized for nonmedical or nonpsychiatric symptoms (Vulnerable Deviants and Protected Deviants) exhibited problem behavior for a much longer time period prior to hospitalization. They also exhibited a greater quantity of unusual behavior and were more visible within and outside the network. Moreover, their unusual behavior impinged upon and created problems for a greater number of groups in the community, especially the police.

Thus, two distinct patterns appear to be associated with the decision to hospitalize. One involves a "speedy" hospitalization undertaken by networks with greater knowledge of and more favorable attitudes toward mental illness. These networks are inclined to view unusual behaviors in medical-psychiatric terms. The second pattern involves a long period during which many problem behaviors are exhibited by the pre-patient, while the network remains uninclined to think about hospitalization. What appears to precipitate hospitalization decisions by these networks is some change in the structure of the network that reduces its ability to cope with a problem member.

In approximately one third of all the cases examined in this research, the decision to hospitalize appeared to have been influenced by the following conditions: (1) the existence of multiple problems in a network that place undue strain on its ability to cope and sustain members, (2) a decline in the number of network members that results in loss of economic or emotional support, and (3) the intervention of professionals in network affairs that influences or forces the network to consider hospitalization. In each of these circumstances additional pressure was put on the network—pressure to which members were unable to adapt.

Hospital Response to Patients and Their Networks

The next stage in the patient's career occurs with admission to the hospital. It might seem that hospitalization represents a smooth and stable transition from being informally recognized by family and community as having psychological problems to being formally recognized by agencies of the state as having a mental illness. Such a transition would be unimportant if the basic definitions of the patient's problem and the patient's network that existed prior to hospitalization were simply transmitted to the hospital and incorporated into the hospital's understanding and definition of the situation. However, that is not the case.

The hospital's definition of new patients and their social networks is contained in the patient's official hospital record, which starts at admission. The record contains descriptions of the patient's problem that may or may not coincide with the views held by network members. The record may also contain assessments of a patient's social network that can influence future expectations about the possibility of release. Thus, the hospital record may be continuous with the definitions of the situation constructed by network members, or it may represent a new reality consisting of views of the patient and the network that are discontinuous with a prior reality.

Examination of hospital records for information on how the first unusual behaviors of patients are depicted indicated substantial differences from accounts of the behaviors provided by network members. The hospital record, in comparison to the social network, was likely to mention more stereotypical and serious symptoms ("delusions and hallucinations," "assaultive and aggressive behavior"). The record may represent an accurate account by hospital staff of information obtained from the network member involved in the commitment process. It may also represent a tendency for the hospital to emphasize the symptoms that provide greatest justification for hospitalization.

Three of the four patient types had similar patterns of differences between information contained in the patient record and information provided by networks. Only Protected Patients had a pattern of symptoms described similarly in hospital records and in network members' accounts.

The hospital record can also influence the fate of patients by the information it chooses to include about social networks. Negative comments about a patient's family may adversely affect chances for weekend home leaves and may discourage staff from thinking about early release from the hospital. On the other hand, comments that describe a positive, supportive climate in a patient's family may lead hospital staff to see early release as realistic.

A search of patient records for positive and negative comments about social networks revealed that when comments were made they were overwhelmingly negative in content and tone. Only the records of Protected Patients failed to contain a single negative comment; the majority of their records contained positive comment. The long-term significance of comments about social networks is revealed by the fact that patients with records containing positive comments on their family are more likely than patients with negative comments to be released from the hospital in the first year after commitment.

The full significance of the patient's hospital record as a reality-defining instrument has hardly been explored. The evidence provided in this research indicates that organizational records should be considered extremely important to an understanding of the patient's career.

The Hospital Experience

Treatment within the hospital, and the records kept about that treatment, were not uniform across patient types and seemed to be related to the committing symptoms and to the resources of the patient's network. The treatment records associated with Patients were more likely to be complete and to indicate that a variety of treatments—for example, drugs, occupational therapy, and group therapy—had been employed with Patients. A larger number of nursing notes were entered into the hospital records about this same group. In contrast, the records about Deviants were more likely to be incomplete. The records also indicated use of fewer kinds of treatment, and nursing notes were more often missing or incomplete.

The hospital experience may include continued contact with friends and relatives. We expected that second thoughts about the decision to hospitalize would influence the frequency of interaction. However, most networks had no second thoughts. There were, nonetheless, differences across the patient types as to time spent with social networks. Protected Patients went on the largest number of leaves and were out of the hospital for the longest periods of time.

Release

Whether a patient is released appears to be related to patient type. That is, release is related to the way in which a network has defined the patient's symptoms as well as to the structure and content of the network. The Protected Patients and Vulnerable Patients in our study followed a career path likely to end in release. Vulnerable Deviants and Protected Deviants were less likely to be released. Moreover, among the nondischarged patients, Vulnerable Deviants had been hospitalized longer. Factors associated with Patients (Vulnerable and Protected)—for example, ties to the patient, closeness among network members, social distance, and lack of fear of violence—were also associated with discharge. However, these factors were not associated with discharge among Vulnerable Deviants.

Theoretical Implications

In this section we discuss the theoretical implications of this study, drawing attention to social networks. Recognizing the significance of social networks leads us to reassess the role of symptoms and resources for the career of mental patients. In addition, we identify multiplexity as an important property of social networks.

Significance of Social Networks

The guiding hypothesis for the present research has been that the properties of social networks help to shape the behavior of constituent members. A social network is a set of direct and indirect ties among a defined group of persons. The configuration of ties, as well as their content, has consequences for the constituent units of the networks. Thus, individual members of a social network may be influenced by persons with whom they have only an indirect tie. The network is composed of individuals, but its properties cannot be reduced to the properties of individuals or pairs of individuals.

We applied the network hypothesis to the question of how persons become hospitalized for mental illness. We examined different stages in the patient's career to demonstrate the plausibility of using network analysis to understand what happens to patients at each stage. There is clear evidence that knowledge of the properties of social networks helps to increase understanding of the social processes involved in defining someone as having a mental illness and in deciding upon hospitalization. Such knowledge also increases understanding of a patient's hospital experiences.

Of particular significance in this research is the way in which a network perspective leads us to modify the central ideas of the medical-psychiatric and societal reaction perspectives. The symptoms exhibited by patients (a central idea of the medical-psychiatric perspective), as well as patients' resources (a central idea of the societal reaction perspective), remain important factors in a patient's career, but in significantly modified form.

A patient's symptoms are important, not because they are clues to a particular illness, but because they have been selected by the network as the way to define the problem behaviors of one of its members. Symptoms are definitions imposed on a patient's unusual behavior, and they have implications for how the network and the hospital respond to the patient. When a network imposes medical-psychiatric definitions, it is responding in part to observed problem behaviors (which are many and varied) and in part to its own cognitive and attitudinal constructs concerning mental illness and mental patients. Having chosen medical-psychiatric symptoms to make sense of observed problem behaviors, the network has automatically adopted an illness model that has built-in expectations of treatment and cure. When the network decides upon hospitalization, it does so with an expectation that the patient will be cured and eventually released from the hospital.

When a patient with medical-psychiatric symptoms enters the hospital, the staff responds in a relatively ordered and standardized way to the symptoms because the hospital also embraces the illness model. Thus, treatment is applied with the expectation that symptoms have an onset and a course and that remission of symptoms can follow treatment. Patients with certain symptoms cause the hospital's medical and psychiatric professionals to become more involved. The professional staff justifies its own expertise and contributes to its sense of self-worth by treating and releasing some of the patients that enter the organization. The existence of very high patient-staff ratios means that only a small number of patients will be "selected" for treatment and release. The patients selected are the ones who will provide the best "fit" between their symptoms and the staff's expertise.

It should be clear that no necessary scientific connection must exist among symptoms, treatment, and the remission of symptoms.

All that is required for the release of a patient is a shared definition of the situation by networks and hospitals and an agreement about the potential for treatment and remission for patients with medical-psychiatric symptoms.

In the case of patients whose symptoms are defined by their networks in nonmedical or nonpsychiatric terms, hospitalization does not automatically connote the same sequence of treatment-remission-release that exists with the illness model. The problems of Deviants are expressed in aggression, excessive drinking, wife beating, or sexual perversion. In the mind of the network, the solution may not be treatment but simply removal from the community.

The hospital tends to look upon the problem behaviors of Deviants with a mixture of moral and medical judgement. Family violence and incest are often felt by hospital staff to be morally objectionable, and they often attribute responsibility for such acts to the patient. Patients are therefore "blamed" for what they have done, while patients with delusions and hallucinations are not held responsible for their symptoms. The consequence of this reaction is that the hospital responds to the patient not in a treatment mode but in a custody mode.

A network perspective is also significant in connection with the idea that a patient's status resources influence whether hospitalization occurs. The societal reaction approach made an important contribution to an understanding of the hospitalization decision by its emphasis upon the role of resources in shaping the decision. However, the societal reaction perspective focused on the status resources of the patient as they functioned to "protect" persons from being hospitalized or to make them vulnerable to hospitalization. Thus, this perspective is important because it specifies the theoretical role of resources. However, the locus of the resources is misplaced. The important point is not the resources of individuals but the resources available to the social networks out of which patients come. The social networks examined in this study revealed different capabilities for support of their members, and these capabilities had important consequences for the patient's career. Some networks were more capable than others of acting in concert, of transmitting information, and of providing emotional support. Networks with these social and emotional resources behaved in a manner different from those without such resources at each stage in the patient's career. Networks with resources not only were more supportive of patients, they were also defined in hospital records as having such capabilities.

It should be clear that our view of network resources does not emphasize economic resources. We are not contrasting working-class and middle-class networks when we speak of networks with and without resources. Almost all the networks in this study had extremely limited economic resources, but each had different capacities for mobilizing and applying human resources.

Thus, future research on the career of the mental patient should concentrate on the different kinds of resources available to networks. It should also look at some of the properties of networks, such as the density of ties among members, as resources available to members. Other properties, such as frequency of contact among members, may not necessarily be resources but may facilitate the flow of resources within the network.

Strength of Multiplex Ties

Our research thus far suggested that social networks are important for increasing our understanding of the career of the mental patient. Networks influence the way in which the problem behaviors of members are defined and dealt with. They also have different kinds of social and emotional resources—that is, capabilities for supporting members in time of need. The concrete properties of networks that were considered in this research included the density of ties among members, the content of ties among members and the patient, the involvement of nonfamily members in the network, and the structure of leadership. Many of these concrete properties can be traced to a more general property of networks that may be of central importance in determining the network's capability of supporting its members—that is, the extent of simplex ties in comparison to multiplex ties.[1] *Simplex ties* exist in a network where members are all tied to one another on a single basis, such as kinship, and where all possible pairs of members have a direct tie. If one network member has a close friend who also knows another member of the network but does not know all the members, then the network ties become more complex. The network now has two strands, kinship and friendship, and members who are linked indirectly. *A* has a tie with *B* and with *C*, but *B* does not have a tie with *C*. The relationship of *A* with *B* can therefore be influenced by someone with whom *B* is tied only indirectly.

Multiplex ties exist in networks that have several different bases of ties among members, such as kinship, friendship, work ties, or membership in the same civic organizations. In short, multiplex networks are many-stranded. They contain members who are directly tied to a subset of all members and who therefore have indirect ties with remaining members.

If we combine the property of multiplex ties with the properties of dense ties and network closeness, we can provide a theoretical explanation for some of the findings uncovered in this research. The social networks associated with Protected Patients appear to come very close to exemplifying the three network properties we have identified. The discussion of the different characteristics of networks in Chapter 3 indicated that Protected Patients' networks were both dense and close. To these characteristics we can now add multiplex ties stemming from the existence of kinship, friendship, and occupational "strands" of network member relationships. Let us consider some of the propositions that can be derived from these network properties and the extent of their explanatory power.

1. *In multiplex networks the problems of any member have greater consequences for members than in simplex networks.* The social networks of Protected Patients act more quickly and positively to obtain medical-psychiatric assistance for their members and to hospitalize them. A network member with a problem has the potential for disrupting kinship, friendship, and work ties (among others) and thereby for affecting a larger number of network members.

2. *Dense networks are more likely to have a consensus on expectations about member behavior than less dense networks.* Networks of Protected Patients exhibit greater agreement on the unusual behaviors exhibited by their members, the time of occurrence of those behaviors, and their perceived seriousness. The greater frequency of interaction in dense networks provides the basis for consensual norms and their consistent application to the behavior of members.

3. *Dense and close networks are more likely to exert pressure on network members to conform to expectations and to support each other in time of need than networks whose members interact infrequently and with weaker emotional ties.* Patients from dense and close networks are dealt with more swiftly by network members after initial unusual behaviors have been observed. Direct efforts are made by the network to modify behavior by exerting pressure on the problem member or by seeking professional help. Such networks are also more likely to have someone identified as "close" to the patient and are more likely to report that the patient agreed with the network's views on the need for hospitalization.

4. *Multiplex networks, because of the greater complexity of member relationships, are more likely to develop an instrumental role structure and to make decisions on matters of concern to the network.* The existence of an agreed-upon leadership and decision-making role structure in multiplex networks is an important factor in enabling networks to move quickly to hospitalize members. Ability to take concerted action may also be responsible for the greater probability that patients from these networks will be released from the hospital. Resources in the network can be mobilized more quickly and with greater certainty; therefore, hospital staff can consider release planning for patients from these networks.

Multiplex networks' higher degree of interdependence and communication among members results in greater sensitivity on the part of network members to disruptive behaviors. These factors are also related to the enforcement of behavioral expectations for network members and to the provision of support when needed. The importance of multiplex ties in social networks is demonstrated by the way in which networks that possess such ties affect the career of the mental patient.

Practical Implications

Although the research reported in this book was not conducted for the specific purpose of developing applied or practical results, a number of things learned from the research may be of value to mental health professionals. First, the research reaffirms the importance for mental health professionals of viewing patients within their social context generally and within their social networks specifically. The medical-psychiatric view of mental illness, with its emphasis on symptoms, disease, and the individual patient, has long dominated the thinking of mental health professionals. Learning to think in network terms would lead professionals to ask different questions about how people get into hospitals, what happens to them in the hospital, and what their chances are for getting out and staying out of the hospital.

All too often community mental health facilities are microcosms of mental hospitals, where out-patients come to receive medication or individual counseling. The focus of such treatment is on the individual patient rather than on the patient and his or her social network. Professionals working in community mental health settings would do well to try to work with the entire social network of a person with problems. The result could be avoidance of commitment for persons who could remain out of the hospital with the right kind of professional and network support.

A focus on the patient as an isolated individual is also found in the recent large-scale effort at decarceration of the mentally ill. Thousands of mental patients have been released from hospitals only to find themselves alone and without social support in many urban centers. The need for community support systems for former mental patients is widely recognized; however, more concerted attempts are necessary to develop and sustain local support systems.

A final recommendation that follows from this research is directed toward professionals working in mental hospitals. If all efforts to keep people out of hospitals and in their social networks fail, then a major attempt should be made to work with the social networks of recently committed persons. Involving the social networks might include modest efforts to encourage hospital visits by network members—perhaps even to provide transportation for them. In addition, more organized efforts might be made to encourage extended home visits while continuing to provide support to the patient and the network. A more ambitious effort would involve hospitals working with community mental health specialists to provide assistance to the networks of patients. For example, the hospital might provide advice on how the network can be more effective in developing and using its resources for the benefit of all members. Mental health specialists might also work with a number of patient networks to better prepare them to use community resources that are either unknown to them or denied to them by community agencies. Finally, professionals might also work with the patient to develop new or additional sources of help and support.

In our society people are expected either to cope alone with what they face or to depend on experts for assistance. But dependence renders them ever more vulnerable and incapable of solving their own problems. The significance of networks is their potential for developing social and emotional strengths that will make people better able to deal with the society in which they live.

Endnote

1. The concept of multiplexity as applied to networks is attributed to the British social anthropologist Max Gluckman. The term has been discussed most fruitfully by J. Clyde Mitchell, "The Concept and Use of Social Networks," in Mitchell, ed., *Social Networks in Urban Situations* (Manchester, England: Manchester University Press, 1969); Bruce Kapferer, "Norms and the Manipulation of Relationships in a Work Context," in Mitchell, *Social Networks*; and J.A. Barnes, "Network Analysis: Orienting Notion, Rigorous Technique, or Substantive Field of Study," in P.W. Holland and S. Leinhardt, *Perspectives on Social Network Research* (New York: Academic Press, 1979). The most important theoretical discussion of network ties, including multiplexity, is provided by Mark Granovetter, "The Strength of Weak Ties," *American Journal of Sociology* 78 (May 1973):1360–80).

APPENDICES

Appendix A

SUMMARY DATA

Table A.1 Frequency of Reported Unusual Behaviors for Patients for Each Network within Patient Types

	Physical Problems	Inter-personal Problems	Unusual Ideas	Role Failure	Aggres-sion	Norm Viola-tions
Patient Type I: Vulnerable Patients						
Network #01	−	+	−	+	+	−
06	−	−	+	−	+	−
08	−	+	+	+	−	−
09	+	+	−	+	+	−
10	−	−	−	−	−	−
16	+	−	+	+	−	−
25	−	+	+	−	−	−
26	−	+	−	−	−	−
29	−	+	+	−	+	+
30	+	−	+	+	−	+
42	−	−	−	−	−	+
43	+	+	+	+	−	−
44	−	−	+	−	−	−
49	+	+	−	+	+	−
Patient Type II: Vulnerable Deviants						
Network #03	+	−	−	+	−	+
07	+	+	+	+	+	−
12	+	+	+	+	+	+
13	−	−	−	−	+	−
14	+	+	−	+	+	−
17	−	+	+	−	+	+
18	+	+	−	+	+	+
19	−	+	+	+	+	−

Table A.1   (continued)

	Physical Problems	Inter-personal Problems	Unusual Ideas	Role Failure	Aggres-sion	Norm Viola-tions
20	+	+	−	−	−	−
21	−	−	−	+	−	−
24	−	+	+	+	−	+
28	−	−	−	−	−	−
32	−	+	−	+	−	+
33	+	+	−	−	−	−
34	−	−	+	−	−	−
37	+	−	−	−	−	+
38	−	+	+	−	+	−
39	−	−	−	−	−	−
41	−	−	−	−	−	+

Patient Type III: Protected Patients

Network	Physical Problems	Inter-personal Problems	Unusual Ideas	Role Failure	Aggres-sion	Norm Viola-tions
#02	−	−	−	−	−	−
04	−	+	+	+	+	+
05	+	+	+	−	+	+
11	+	−	+	−	−	+
15	−	+	−	−	−	+
22	−	+	+	+	−	+
35	−	−	−	−	+	−
36	+	+	−	−	−	+
46	+	−	−	−	+	−
48	−	−	−	+	−	−

Patient Type IV: Protected Deviants

Network	Physical Problems	Inter-personal Problems	Unusual Ideas	Role Failure	Aggres-sion	Norm Viola-tions
#23	−	−	−	−	−	−
27	+	−	−	+	+	+
31	−	−	−	−	−	−
47	+	+	+	+	−	−

Note: + equals rate of reported unusual behavior is above the mean rate for that behavior for all networks within a patient type.
      − equals rate of reported unusual behavior is below the mean rate for that behavior for all networks within a patient type.

Table A.2   Number of Networks and Percentage of Network Members Reporting that Patient Accepted Definition of Illness and Need for Hospitalization

| | Percentage of Network Members, by Patient Type | | | | | | | | | | | |
| | Vulnerable Patients | | | Vulnerable Deviants | | | Protected Patients | | | Protected Deviants | | |
	−50%	50%+	100%	−50%	50%+	100%	−50%	50%+	100%	−50%	50%+	100%
Number of networks stating: "Patient agreed he/she had a mental illness."	3	5	6	7	8	4	3	3	4	3	1	0
Percentage		79%			63%			70%			25%	
Number of networks stating: "Patient agreed hospitalization was necessary."	3	6	5	9	6	4	2	4	4	4	0	0
Percentage		79%			53%			80%			0%	

TOLERANCE FOR DEVIANCE

Listed below are descriptions of six different people. Read each description and answer the questions following each description.*

1. I'm thinking of a man—let's call him Frank Jones—who is very suspicious; he doesn't trust anybody, and he's sure that everybody is against him. Sometimes he thinks that people he sees on the street are talking about him or following him around. A couple of times now he has beaten up men who didn't even know him. The other night he began to curse his wife terribly; then he hit her and threatened to kill her because, he said, she was working against him, too, just like everyone else.

    A. Check the *one* category below that you think best describes [Frank Jones].

    _____ There may be something wrong with him, but it's not mental illness and not serious.

    _____ He has mental illness, but it's not serious.

    _____ He hasn't got mental illness, but it is serious.

    _____ He has a serious mental illness.

    B. Check the *one* category below that describes the kind of help you think that [Frank Jones] should get.

    _____ He should be admitted to a mental hospital.

    _____ He should probably get help outside the hospital from a doctor who specializes in mental illness.

---

* *Note:* Questions A and B and the possible responses are the same for descriptions 1–6. Therefore, they are listed only after the first description.

_____ He should get help from his family and friends.
_____ He just needs a rest, like a vacation.
_____ He doesn't need any help; he can get over it himself.

2. Now here's a young woman in her twenties; let's call her Betty Smith. She has never had a job, and she doesn't seem to want to go out and look for one. She is a very quiet girl, she doesn't talk much to anyone—even her own family—and she acts like she is afraid of people, especially young men her own age. She won't go out with anyone, and whenever someone comes to visit her family, she stays in her room until they leave. She just stays by herself and daydreams all the time, and shows no interest in anything or anybody.

3. Here's another kind of man; we can call him George Brown. He has a good job and is doing pretty well at it. Most of the time he gets along all right with people, but he is always very touchy and he always loses his temper quickly if things aren't going his way or if people find fault with him. He worries a lot about little things, and he seems to be moody and unhappy all the time. Everything is going along all right for him, but he can't sleep nights, brooding about the past and worrying about things that *might be* wrong.

4. How about Bill Williams? He never seems to be able to hold a job very long because he drinks so much. Whenever he has money in his pocket, he goes on a spree; he stays out till all hours drinking and never seems to care what happens to his wife and children. Sometimes he feels very bad about the way he treats his family; he begs his wife to forgive him and promises to stop drinking, but he always goes off again.

5. Here's a different sort of girl—let's call her Mary White. She seems happy and cheerful; she's pretty, has a good job, and is engaged to marry a nice young man. She has loads of friends; everybody likes her, and she's always busy and active. However, she just can't leave the house without going back to see whether she left the gas stove lit or not. And she always goes back again just to make sure she locked the door. And one other thing about her: She's afraid to ride up and down in elevators; she just won't go anyplace where she'd have to ride in an elevator to get there.

6. Now I'd like to describe a twelve-year-old boy—Bobby Grey. He's bright enough and in good health, and he comes from a comfortable home. But his father and mother have found out that he's been telling lies for a long time now. He's been stealing things from stores and taking money from his mother's purse, and he has been playing truant, staying away from school whenever he can. His parents are very upset about the way he acts, but he pays no attention to them.

Appendix C

RESEARCH DESIGN

The objectives of this research required a sample of patients and their social networks. Patients had to be first admissions, between eighteen and fifty-five years of age, and hospitalized for a broad class of functional disorders. Social networks involved all persons closely associated with the patient in the months prior to hospitalization or involved in the commitment decision.

We obtained the cooperation of two large state mental hospitals, one serving a predominantly rural catchment area and the other an urban area. A contact person in the hospital would call the project office each time a patient with the required characteristics was admitted. The contact would provide the patient's name and the name of the committing party or closest relative. A member of the project staff then contacted the committing party or closest relative for an interview. The names of other persons closely involved with the patient was the first information obtained. A formal recorded interview covered the following topics: relationships among network members, description of first unusual behavior of the patient, description of the commitment decision, and discussion of specific events and persons involved in the commitment decision. Following the formal interview, the respondent completed a series of questionnaires involving tolerance for deviance, knowledge of mental illness, attitudes toward the mentally ill, and all unusual behaviors exhibited by the patient prior to hospitalization.

All subsequent interviews for each patient's network followed from the names provided by the first person and by each person interviewed after the first person. This "snowball sample" procedure very quickly yielded a redundant set of names, which became the patient's social network. Interviews were conducted in the respondents' homes and were recorded on tape.

At the end of the second year of the project, the hospital records of each patient were read. Selected information was recorded and later coded. This information was added to the data record of each patient and each network.

In the original plan of the research, we intended to obtain a sample of about sixty patients, half from each hospital. However, the rate of first admissions was lower than anticipated, and we had to terminate data collection at forty-seven patients.

INDEX